A Treatise on Nature and Grace

A Treatise on Nature and Grace

St. Augustine

A Treatise on Nature and Grace

© Lighthouse Publishing 2018

Written by: St. Augustine (Nov.13 354 – Aug.28 430)
Translated by Peter Holmes and Robert Ernest Wallis
Revised by: Professor Benjamin B. Warfield, D.D
Updated into Modern U.S English by A.M. Overett (b. 1960)

All rights reserved. Without limiting the rights under copyright reserved above, no part of this publication may be reproduced, stored in a retrieval system, or transmitted, in any form or by any means (electronic, mechanical, photocopying, recording or otherwise), without the prior written permission of the copyright owner of this book.

Published by
Lighthouse Christian Publishing
SAN 257-4330
5531 Dufferin Drive
Savage, Minnesota, 55378
United States of America

www.lighthousechristianpublishing.com

EXTRACT FROM AUGUSTIN'S "RETRACTATIONS,"

Book II. Chap. 42,

ON THE FOLLOWING TREATISE, "DE NATURA ET GRATIA."

"At that time also there came into my hands a certain book of Pelagius', in which he defends, with all the argumentative skill he could muster, the nature of man, in opposition to the grace of God whereby the unrighteous is justified and we become Christians. The treatise which contains my reply to him, and in which I defend grace, not indeed as in opposition to nature, but as that which liberates and controls nature, I have entitled On Nature and Grace. In this work sundry short passages, which were quoted by Pelagius as the words of the Roman bishop and martyr, Xystus, were vindicated by myself as if they really were the words of this Sixtus. For this I thought them at the time; but I afterwards discovered, that Sextus the heathen philosopher, and not Xystus the Christian bishop, was their author. This treatise of mine begins with the words: 'The book which you sent me.'"

A TREATISE ON NATURE AND GRACE, AGAINST PELAGIUS;

BY AURELIUS AUGUSTIN, BISHOP OF HIPPO;

Contained in One Book, addressed to timasius and jacobus.

WRITTEN IN THE YEAR OF OUR LORD 415. ———

He begins with a statement of what is to be investigated concerning nature and grace; he shows that nature, as propagated from the flesh of the sinful Adam, being no longer what God made it at first,—faultless and sound,—requires the aid of grace, in order that it may be redeemed from the wrath of God and regulated for the perfection of righteousness: that the penal fault of nature leads to a most righteous retribution: whilst grace itself is not rendered to any deserts of ours, but is given gratuitously; and they who are not delivered by it are justly condemned. He afterwards refutes, with answers on every several point, a work by Pelagius, who supports this self-same nature in opposition to grace; among other things especially, in his desire to recommend the opinion that a man can live without sin, he contended that nature had not been weakened and changed by sin; for, otherwise, the matter of sin (which he thinks absurd) would be its punishment, if the sinner were weakened to such a degree that he committed more sin. He goes on to enumerate sundry righteous men both of the Old and of the New Testaments: deeming these to have been free from sin, he alleged the possibility of not sinning to be inherent in man; and this he attributed to God's grace, because God is the author of that nature in which is inseparably inherent this possibility of avoiding sin. Towards the end of this treatise there is an examination of sundry extracts from old writers, which Pelagius adduced in support of his views, and expressly from Hilary, Ambrose, and even Augustin himself.

Chapter 1 [I.]—The Occasion of Publishing This Work; What God's Righteousness is.

The book which you sent to me, my beloved sons, Timasius and Jacobus, I have read through hastily, but not indifferently, omitting only the few points which are plain enough to everybody; and I saw in it a man inflamed with most ardent zeal against those, who, when in their sins they ought to censure human will, are more forward in accusing the nature of men, and thereby endeavor to excuse themselves. He shows too great a fire against this evil, which even authors of secular literature have severely censured with the exclamation: "The human race falsely complains of its own nature!" This same sentiment your author also has strongly insisted upon, with all the powers of his talent. I fear, however, that he will chiefly help those "who have a zeal for God, but not according to knowledge," who, "being ignorant of God's righteousness, and going about to establish their own righteousness, have not submitted themselves to the righteousness of God." Now, what the righteousness of God is, which is spoken of here, he immediately afterwards explains by adding: "For Christ is the end of the law for righteousness to everyone that believeth." This righteousness of God, therefore, lies not in the commandment of the law, which excites fear, but in the aid afforded by the grace of Christ, to which alone the fear of the law, as of a schoolmaster, usefully conducts. Now, the man who understands this understands why he is a Christian. For "If righteousness came by the law, then Christ is dead in vain." If, however He did not die in vain, in Him only is the ungodly man justified, and to him, on believing in Him who justifies the ungodly, faith is reckoned for righteousness. For all men have sinned and come short of the glory of God, being justified freely by His blood. But all those who do not think themselves to belong to the "all who have sinned and fall short of the glory of God," have of course no need to become Christians, because "they that be whole need not a physician, but they that are sick;" whence it is, that He came not to call the righteous, but sinners to repentance.

Chapter 2 [II.]—Faith in Christ Not Necessary to Salvation, if a Man Without It Can Lead a Righteous Life.

Therefore the nature of the human race, generated from the flesh of the one transgressor, if it is self-sufficient for fulfilling the law and for perfecting righteousness, ought to be sure of its reward, that is, of everlasting life, even if in any nation or at any former time faith in the blood of Christ was unknown to it. For God is not so unjust as to defraud righteous persons of the reward of righteousness, because there has not been announced to them the mystery of Christ's divinity and humanity, which was manifested in the flesh. For how could they believe what they had not heard of; or how could they hear without a preacher? For "faith cometh by hearing, and hearing by the word of Christ." But I say (adds he): Have they not heard? "Yea, verily; their sound went out into all the earth, and their words unto the ends of the world." Before, however, all this had been accomplished, before the actual preaching of the gospel reaches the ends of all the earth—because there are some remote nations still (although it is said they are very few) to whom the preached gospel has not found its way,—what must human nature do, or what has it done—for it had either not heard that all this was to take place, or has not yet learnt that it was accomplished—but believe in God who made heaven and earth, by whom also it perceived by nature that it had been itself created, and lead a right life, and thus accomplish His will, uninstructed with any faith in the death and resurrection of Christ? Well, if this could have been done, or can still be done, then for my part I must say what the apostle said regarding the law: "Then Christ died in vain." For if he said this about the law, which only the nation of the Jews received, how much more justly may it be said of the law of nature, which the whole human race has received, "If righteousness come by nature, then Christ died in vain." If, however, Christ did not die in vain, then human nature cannot by any means be justified and redeemed from God's most righteous wrath—in a word, from punishment—except by faith and the sacrament of the blood of Christ.

Chapter 3 [III.]—Nature Was Created Sound and Whole; It Was Afterwards Corrupted by Sin.

Man's nature, indeed, was created at first faultless and without any sin; but that nature of man in which everyone is born from Adam, now wants the Physician, because it is not sound. All good qualities, no doubt, which it still possesses in its make, life, senses, intellect, it has of the Most High God, its Creator and Maker. But the flaw, which darkens and weakens all those natural goods, so that it has need of illumination and healing, it has not contracted from its blameless Creator—but from that original sin, which it committed by free will. Accordingly, criminal nature has its part in most righteous punishment. For, if we are now newly created in Christ, we were, for all that, children of wrath, even as others, "but God, who is rich in mercy, for His great love wherewith He loved us, even when we were dead in sins, hath quickened us together with Christ, by whose grace we were saved."

Chapter 4 [IV.]—Free Grace.

This grace, however, of Christ, without which neither infants nor adults can be saved, is not rendered for any merits, but is given gratis, because which it is also called grace. "Being justified," says the apostle, "freely through His blood." Whence they, who are not liberated through grace, either because they are not yet able to hear, or because they are unwilling to obey; or again because they did not receive, at the time when they were unable on account of youth to hear, that bath of regeneration, which they might have received and through which they might have been saved, are indeed justly condemned; because they are not without sin, either that which they have derived from their birth, or that which they have added from their own misconduct. "For all have sinned"—whether in Adam or in themselves— "and come short of the glory of God."

Chapter 5 [V.]—It Was a Matter of Justice that All Should Be Condemned.

The entire mass, therefore, incurs penalty and if the deserved punishment of condemnation were rendered to all, it would without doubt be righteously rendered. They, therefore, who are delivered therefrom by grace are called, not vessels of their own merits, but "vessels of mercy." But of whose mercy, if not His who sent Christ Jesus into the world to save sinners, whom He foreknew, and foreordained, and called, and justified, and glorified? Now, who could be so madly insane as to fail to give ineffable thanks to the Mercy which liberates whom it would? The man who correctly appreciated the whole subject could not possibly blame the justice of God in wholly condemning all men whatsoever.

Chapter 6 [VI.]—The Pelagians Have Very Strong and Active Minds.

If we are simply wise according to the Scriptures, we are not compelled to dispute against the grace of Christ, and to make statements attempting to show that human nature both requires no Physician, —in infants, because it is whole and sound; and in adults, because it is able to suffice for itself in attaining righteousness, if it will. Men no doubt seem to urge acute opinions on these points, but it is only word-wisdom, by which the cross of Christ is made of none effect. This, however, "is not the wisdom which descended from above." The words which follow in the apostle's statement I am unwilling to quote; for we would rather not be thought to do an injustice to our friends, whose very strong and active minds we should be sorry to see running in a perverse, instead of an upright, course.

Chapter 7 [VII.]—He Proceeds to Confute the Work of Pelagius; He Refrains as Yet from Mentioning Pelagius' Name.

However ardent, then, is the zeal which the author of the book you have forwarded to me entertains against those who find a defense for their sins in the infirmity of human nature; not less, nay even much greater, should be our eagerness in preventing all attempts to render the cross of Christ of none effect. Of none effect, however, it is rendered, if it be contended that by any other means than by Christ's own sacrament it is possible to attain to righteousness and everlasting life. This is actually done in the book to which I refer—I will not say by its author wittingly, lest I should express the judgment that he ought not to be accounted even a Christian, but, as I rather believe, unconsciously. He has done it, no doubt, with much power; I only wish that the ability he has displayed were sound and less like that which insane persons are accustomed to exhibit.

Chapter 8. —A Distinction Drawn by Pelagius Between the Possible and Actual.

For he first of all makes a distinction: "It is one thing," says he, "to inquire whether a thing can be, which has respect to its possibility only; and another thing, whether or not it is." This distinction, nobody doubts, is true enough; for it follows that whatever is, was able to be; but it does not therefore follow that what is able to be, also is. Our Lord, for instance, raised Lazarus; He unquestionably was able to do so. But inasmuch as He did not raise up Judas must we therefore contend that He was unable to do so? He certainly was able, but He would not. For if He had been willing, He could have affected this too. For the Son quickened whomsoever He will. Observe, however, what he means by this distinction, true and manifest enough in itself, and what he endeavors to make out of it. "We are treating," says he, "of possibility only; and to pass from this to something else, except in the case of some certain fact, we deem to be a very serious and extraordinary process." This idea he turns over again and again, in many ways and at great length, so that no one would suppose that he was inquiring about any other point than the possibility of not committing sin. Among the many passages in which he treats of this subject, occurs the following: "I once more repeat my position: I say that it is possible for a man to be without sin. What do you say? That it is impossible for a man to be without sin? But I do not say," he adds, "that there is a man without sin; nor do you say, that there is not a man without sin. Our contention is about what is possible, and not possible; not about what is, and is not." He then enumerates certain passages of Scripture, which are usually alleged in opposition to them, and insists that they have nothing to do with the question, which is really in dispute, as to the possibility or impossibility of a man's being without sin. This is what he says: "No man indeed is clean from pollution; and, There is no man that sinned not; and, There is not a just man upon the earth; and, There is none that doeth good. There are these and similar passages in Scripture," says he, "but they testify to the point of not being, not of not being able; for by testimonies of this sort it is shown what kind of persons certain men were at such and such a time, not that they were unable to be something else. Whence they are justly found to be blameworthy. If, however, they had been of such a character, simply because they were unable to be anything else, they are free from blame."

Chapter 9 [VIII.]—Even They Who Were Not Able to Be Justified are Condemned.

See what he has said. I, however, affirm that an infant born in a place where it was not possible for him to be admitted to the baptism of Christ, and being overtaken by death, was placed in such circumstances, that is to say, died without the bath of regeneration, because it was not possible for him to be otherwise. He would therefore absolve him, and, despite the Lord's sentence, open to him the kingdom of heaven. The apostle, however, does not absolve him, when he says: "By one man sin entered into the world, and death by sin; by which death passed upon all men, for that all have sinned." Rightly, therefore, by virtue of that condemnation which runs throughout the mass, is he not admitted into the kingdom of heaven, although he was not only not a Christian, but was unable to become one.

Chapter 10 [IX.]—He Could Not Be Justified, Who Had Not Heard of the Name of Christ; Rendering the Cross of Christ of None Effect.

But they say: "He is not condemned; because the statement that all sinned in Adam, was not made because of the sin which is derived from one's birth, but because of imitation of him." If, therefore, Adam is said to be the author of all the sins which followed his own, because he was the first sinner of the human race, then how is it that Abel, rather than Christ, is not placed at the head of all the righteous, because he was the first righteous man? But I am not speaking of the case of an infant. I take the instance of a young man, or an old man, who has died in a region where he could not hear of the name of Christ. Well, could such a man have become righteous by nature and free will; or could he not? If they contend that he could, then see what it is to render the cross of Christ of none effect, to contend that any man without it, can be justified by the law of nature and the power of his will. We may here also say, then is Christ dead in vain forasmuch as all might accomplish so much as this, even if He had never died; and if they should be unrighteous, they would be so because they wished to be, not because they were unable to be righteous. But even though a man could not be justified at all without the grace of Christ, he would absolve him, if he dared, in accordance with his words, to the effect that, "if a man were of such a character, because he could not possibly have been of any other, he would be free from all blame."

Chapter 11 [X.]—Grace Subtly Acknowledged by Pelagius.

He then starts an objection to his own position, as if, indeed, another person had raised it, and says: "'A man,' you will say, 'may possibly be [without sin]; but it is by the grace of God.'" He then at once subjoins the following, as if in answer to his own suggestion: "I thank you for your kindness, because you are not merely content to withdraw your opposition to my statement, which you just now opposed, or barely to acknowledge it; but you actually go so far as to approve it. For to say, 'A man may possibly, but by this or by that,' is in fact nothing else than not only to assent to its possibility, but also to show the mode and condition of its possibility. Nobody, therefore, gives a better assent to the possibility of anything than the man who allows the condition thereof; because, without the thing itself, it is not possible for a condition to be." After this he raises another objection against himself: "But, you will say, 'you here seem to reject the grace of God, inasmuch as you do not even mention it;'" and he then answers the objection: "Now, is it I that reject grace, who by acknowledging the thing must needs also confess the means by which it may be effected, or you, who by denying the thing do undoubtedly also deny whatever may be the means through which the thing is accomplished?" He forgot that he was now answering one who does not deny the thing, and whose objection he had just before set forth in these words: "A man may possibly be [without sin]; but it is by the grace of God." How then does that man deny the possibility, in defense of which his opponent earnestly contends, when he makes the admission to that opponent that "the thing is possible, but only by the grace of God?" That, however, after he is dismissed who already acknowledges the essential thing, he still has a question against those who maintain the impossibility of a man's being without sin, what is it to us? Let him ply his questions against any opponents he pleases, provided he only confesses this, which cannot be denied without the most criminal impiety, that without the grace of God a man cannot be without sin. He says, indeed: "Whether he confesses it to be by grace, or by aid, or by mercy, whatever that be by which a man can be without sin, — everyone acknowledges the thing itself."

Chapter 12 [XI.]—In Our Discussions About Grace, We Do Not Speak of that Which Relates to the Constitution of Our Nature, But to Its Restoration.

I confess to your love, that when I read those words I was filled with a sudden joy, because he did not deny the grace of God by which alone a man can be justified; for it is this which I mainly detest and dread in discussions of this kind. But when I went on to read the rest, I began to have my suspicions, first of all, from the similes he employs. For he says: "If I were to say, man is able to dispute; a bird is able to fly; a hare is able to run; without mentioning at the same time the instruments by which these acts can be accomplished—that is, the tongue, the wings, and the legs; should I then have denied the conditions of the various offices, when I acknowledged the very offices themselves?" It is at once apparent that he has here instanced such things as are by nature efficient; for the members of the bodily structure which are here mentioned are created with natures of such a kind—the tongue, the wings, the legs. He has not here posited any such thing as we wish to have understood by grace, without which no man is justified; for this is a topic which is concerned about the cure, not the constitution, of natural functions. Entertaining, then, some apprehensions, I proceeded to read all the rest, and I soon found that my suspicions had not been unfounded.

Chapter 13 [XII.]—The Scope and Purpose of the Law's Threatenings; "Perfect Wayfarers."

But before I proceed further, see what he has said. When treating the question about the difference of sins, and starting as an objection to himself, what certain persons allege, "that some sins are light by their very frequency, their constant irruption making it impossible that they should be all of them avoided;" he thereupon denied that it was "proper that they should be censured even as light offences, if they cannot possibly be wholly avoided." He of course does not notice the Scriptures of the New Testament, wherein we learn that the intention of the law in its censure is this, that, because of the transgressions which men commit, they may flee for refuge to the grace of the Lord, who has pity upon them— "the schoolmaster" "shutting them up unto the same faith which should afterwards be revealed;" that by it their transgressions may be forgiven, and then not again be committed, by God's assisting grace. The road indeed belongs to all who are progressing in it; although it is they who make a good advance that are called "perfect travelers." That, however, is the height of perfection which admits of no addition, when the goal to which men tend has begun to be possessed.

Chapter 14 [XIII.]—Refutation of Pelagius.

But the truth is, the question which is proposed to him— "Are you even yourself without sin?"—does not really belong to the subject in dispute. What, however, he says,—that "it is rather to be imputed to his own negligence that he is not without sin," is no doubt well spoken; but then he should deem it to be his duty even to pray to God that this faulty negligence get not the dominion over him,—the prayer that a certain man once put up, when he said: "Order my steps according to Thy word, and let not any iniquity have dominion over me,"— lest, whilst relying on his own diligence as on strength of his own, he should fail to attain to the true righteousness either by this way, or by that other method in which, no doubt, perfect righteousness is to be desired and hoped for.

Chapter 15 [XIV.]—Not Everything [of Doctrinal Truth] is Written in Scripture in So Many Words.

That, too, which is said to him, "that it is nowhere written in so many words, A man can be without sin," he easily refutes thus: "That the question here is not in what precise words each doctrinal statement is made." It is perhaps not without reason that, while in several passages of Scripture we may find it said that men are without excuse, it is nowhere found that any man is described as being without sin, except Him only, of whom it is plainly said, that "He knew no sin." Similarly, we read in the passage where the subject is concerning priests: "He was in all points tempted like as we are, only without sin,"— meaning, of course, in that flesh which bore the likeness of sinful flesh, although it was not sinful flesh; a likeness, indeed, which it would not have borne if it had not been in every other respect the same as sinful flesh. How, however, we are to understand this: "Whosoever is born of God doth not commit sin; neither can he sin, for his seed remained in him;" while the Apostle John himself, as if he had not been born of God, or else were addressing men who had not been born of God, lays down this position: "If we say that we have no sin, we deceive ourselves, and the truth is not in us,"—I have already explained, with such care as I was able, in those books which I wrote to Marcellinus on this very subject. It seems, moreover, to me to be an interpretation worthy of acceptance to regard the clause of the above quoted passage: "Neither can he sin," as if it meant: He ought not to commit sin. For who could be so foolish as to say that sin ought to be committed, when, in fact, sin is sin, for no other reason than that it ought not to be committed?

Chapter 16 [XV.]—Pelagius Corrupts a Passage of the Apostle James by Adding a Note of Interrogation.

Now that passage, in which the Apostle James says: "But the tongue can no man tame," does not appear to me to be capable of the interpretation which he would put upon it, when he expounds it, "as if it were written by way of reproach; as much as to say: Can no man then, tame the tongue? As if in a reproachful tone, which would say: You are able to tame wild beasts; cannot you tame the tongue? As if it were an easier thing to tame the tongue than to subjugate wild beasts." I do not think that this is the meaning of the passage. For, if he had meant such an opinion as this to be entertained of the facility of taming the tongue, there would have followed in the sequel of the passage a comparison of that member with the beasts. As it is, however, it simply goes on to say: "The tongue is an unruly evil, full of deadly poison,"—such, of course, as is more noxious than that of beasts and creeping things. For while the one destroys the flesh, the other kills the soul. For, "The mouth that belie slayed the soul." It is not, therefore, as if this is an easier achievement than the taming of beasts that St. James pronounced the statement before us, or would have others utter it; but he rather aims at showing what a great evil in man his tongue is—so great, indeed, that it cannot be tamed by any man, although even beasts are tamable by human beings. And he said this, not with a view to our permitting, through our neglect, the continuance of so great an evil to ourselves, but in order that we might be induced to request the help of divine grace for the taming of the tongue. For he does not say: "None can tame the tongue;" but "No man;" in order that, when it is tamed, we may acknowledge it to be affected by the mercy of God, the help of God, the grace of God. The soul, therefore, should endeavor to tame the tongue, and while endeavoring should pray for assistance; the tongue, too, should beg for the taming of the tongue, —He being the tamer who said to His disciples: "It is not ye that speak, but the Spirit of your Father which speaks in you." Thus, we are warned by the precept to do this, —namely, to make the attempt, and, failing in our own strength, to pray for the help of God.

Chapter 17 [XVI.]—Explanation of This Text Continued.

Accordingly, after emphatically describing the evil of the tongue—saying, among other things: "My brethren, these things ought not so to be"—he at once, after finishing some remarks which arose out of his subject, goes on to add this advice, showing by what help those things would not happen, which (as he said) ought not: "Who is a wise man and endowed with knowledge among you? Let him show out of a good conversation his works with meekness of wisdom. But if ye have bitter envying and strife in your hearts, glory not and lie not against the truth. This wisdom descended not from above, but is earthly, sensual, devilish. For where there is envying and strife, there is confusion and every evil work. But the wisdom that is from above is first pure, then peaceable, gentle, and easy to be entreated, full of mercy and good fruits, without partiality, and without hypocrisy." This is the wisdom which tames the tongue; it descends from above, and springs from no human heart. Will any one, then, dare to divorce it from the grace of God, and with most arrogant vanity places it in the power of man? Why should I pray to God that it be accorded me, if it may be had of man? Ought we not to object to this prayer lest injury be done to free will which is self-sufficient in the possibility of nature for discharging all the duties of righteousness? We ought, then, to object also to the Apostle James himself, who admonishes us in these words: "If any of you lack wisdom, let him ask of God, that giveth to all men liberally, and upbraided not, and it shall be given him; but let him ask in faith, nothing doubting." This is the faith to which the commandments drive us, in order that the law may prescribe our duty and faith accomplish it. For through the tongue, which no man can tame, but only the wisdom which comes down from above, "in many things we all of us offend." For this truth also the same apostle pronounced in no other sense than that in which he afterwards declares: "The tongue no man can tame."

Chapter 18 [XVII.]—Who May Be Said to Be in the Flesh.

There is a passage which nobody could place against these texts with the similar purpose of showing the impossibility of not sinning: "The wisdom of the flesh is enmity against God; for it is not subject to the law of God, neither indeed can be; so then they that are in the flesh cannot please God;" for he here mentions the wisdom of the flesh, not the wisdom which cometh from above: moreover, it is manifest, that in this passage, by the phrase, "being in the flesh," are signified, not those who have not yet quitted the body, but those who live according to the flesh. The question, however, we are discussing does not lie in this point. But what I want to hear from him, if I can, is about those who live according to the Spirit, and who on this account are not, in a certain sense, in the flesh, even while they still live here, — whether they, by God's grace, live according to the Spirit, or are sufficient for themselves, natural capability having been bestowed on them when they were created, and their own proper will besides. Whereas the fulfilling of the law is nothing else than love; and God's love is shed abroad in our hearts, not by our own selves, but by the Holy Ghost which is given to us.

Chapter 19. —Sins of Ignorance; To Whom Wisdom is Given by God on Their Requesting It.

He further treats of sins of ignorance, and says that "a man ought to be very careful to avoid ignorance; and that ignorance is blameworthy for this reason, because it is through his own neglect that a man is ignorant of that which he certainly must have known if he had only applied diligence;" whereas he prefers disputing all things rather than to pray, and say: "Give me understanding, that I may learn Thy commandments." It is, indeed, one thing to have taken no pains to know what sins of negligence were apparently expiated even through divers sacrifices of the law; it is another thing to wish to understand, to be unable, and then to act contrary to the law, through not understanding what it would have done. We are accordingly enjoined to ask of God wisdom, "who giveth to all men liberally;" that is, of course, to all men who ask in such a manner, and to such an extent, as so great a matter requires in earnestness of petition.

Chapter 20 [XVIII.]—What Prayer Pelagius Would Admit to Be Necessary.

He confesses that "sins which have been committed do notwithstanding require to be divinely expiated, and that the Lord must be entreated because of them,"—that is, for the purpose, of course, of obtaining pardon; "because that which has been done cannot," it is his own admission, "be undone," by that "power of nature and will of man" which he talks about so much. From this necessity, therefore, it follows that a man must pray to be forgiven. That a man, however, requires to be helped not to sin, he has nowhere admitted; I read no such admission in this passage; he keeps a strange silence on this subject altogether; although the Lord's Prayer enjoins upon us the necessity of praying both that our debts may be remitted to us, and that we may not be led into temptation, —the one petition entreating that past offences may be atoned for; the other, that future ones may be avoided. Now, although this is never done unless our will be assistant, yet our will alone is not enough to secure its being done; the prayer, therefore, which is offered up to God for this result is neither superfluous nor offensive to the Lord. For what is more foolish than to pray that you may do that which you have it in your own power to do.

Chapter 21 [XIX.]—Pelagius Denies that Human Nature Has Been Depraved or Corrupted by Sin.

You may now see (what bears very closely on our subject) how he endeavors to exhibit human nature, as if it were wholly without fault, and how he struggles against the plainest of God's Scriptures with that "wisdom of word" which renders the cross of Christ of none effect. That cross, however, shall certainly never be made of none effect; rather shall such wisdom be subverted. Now, after we shall have demonstrated this, it may be that God's mercy may visit him, so that he may be sorry that he ever said these things: "We have," he says, "first of all to discuss the position which is maintained, that our nature has been weakened and changed by sin. I think," continues he, "that before all other things we have to inquire what sin is, —some substance, or wholly a name without substance, whereby is expressed not a thing, not an existence, not some sort of a body, but the doing of a wrongful deed." He then adds: "I suppose that this is the case; and if so," he asks, "how could that which lacks all substance have possibly weakened or changed human nature?" Observe, I beg of you, how in his ignorance he struggles to overthrow the most salutary words of the remedial Scriptures: "I said, O Lord, be merciful unto me; heal my soul, for I have sinned against Thee." Now, how can a thing be healed, if it is not wounded nor hurt, nor weakened and corrupted? But, as there is here something to be healed, whence did it receive its injury? You hear [the Psalmist] confessing the fact; what need is there of discussion? He says: "Heal my soul." Ask him how that which he wants to be healed became injured, and then listen to his following words: "Because I have sinned against Thee." Let him, however, put a question, and ask what he deemed a suitable inquiry, and say: "O you who exclaim, Heal my soul, for I have sinned against Thee! pray tell me what sin is? Some substance, or wholly a name without substance, whereby is expressed, not a thing, not an existence, not some sort of a body, but merely the doing of a wrongful deed?" Then the other returns for answer: "It is even as you say; sin is not some substance; but under its name there is merely expressed the doing of a wrongful deed." But he rejoins: "Then why cry out, Heal my soul, for I have sinned against Thee? How could that have possibly corrupted your soul which lacks all substance?" Then would the other, worn out with the anguish of his wound, in order to avoid being diverted from prayer by the discussion, briefly answer and say: "Go from me, I beseech you; rather discuss the point, if you can, with Him who said: 'They that are whole need no physician, but they that are sick; I am not come to call the righteous, but sinners,'" —in which words, of course, He designated the righteous as the whole, and sinners as the sick.

Chapter 22 [XX.]—How Our Nature Could Be Vitiated by Sin, Even Though It Be Not a Substance.

Now, do you not perceive the tendency and direction of this controversy? Even to render of none effect the Scripture where it is said "Thou shalt call His name Jesus, for He shall save His people from their sins." For how is He to save where there is no malady? For the sins, from which this gospel says Christ's people have to be saved, are not substances, and according to this writer are incapable of corrupting. O brother, how good a thing it is to remember that you are a Christian! To believe, might perhaps be enough; but still, since you persist in discussion, there is no harm, nay there is even benefit, if a firm faith precedes it; let us not suppose, then, that human nature cannot be corrupted by sin, but rather, believing, from the inspired Scriptures, that it is corrupted by sin, let our inquiry be how this could possibly have come about. Since, then, we have already learnt that sin is not a substance, do we not consider, not to mention any other example, that not to eat is also not a substance? Because such abstinence is withdrawal from a substance, inasmuch as food is a substance. To abstain, then, from food is not a substance; and yet the substance of our body, if it does altogether abstain from food, so languishes, is so impaired by broken health, is so exhausted of strength, so weakened and broken with very weariness, that even if it be in any way able to continue alive, it is hardly capable of being restored to the use of that food, by abstaining from which it became so corrupted and injured. In the same way sin is not a substance; but God is a substance, yea the height of substance and only true sustenance of the reasonable creature. The consequence of departing from Him by disobedience, and of inability, through infirmity, to receive what one ought really to rejoice in, you hear from the Psalmist, when he says: "My heart is smitten and withered like grass, since I have forgotten to eat my bread."

Chapter 23 [XXI.]—Adam Delivered by the Mercy of Christ.

But observe how, by specious arguments, he continues to oppose the truth of Holy Scripture. The Lord Jesus, who is called Jesus because He saves His people from their sins, in accordance with this His merciful character, says: "They that be whole need not a physician, but they that are sick; I am come not to call the righteous, but sinners to repentance." Accordingly, His apostle also says: "This is a faithful saying, and worthy of all acceptation, that Christ Jesus came into the world to save sinners." This man, however, contrary to the "faithful saying, and worthy of all acceptation," declares that "this sickness ought not to have been contracted by sins, lest the punishment of sin should amount to this, that more sins should be committed." Now even for infants the help of the Great Physician is sought. This writer asks: "Why seek Him? They are whole for whom you seek the Physician. Not even was the first man condemned to die for any such reason, for he did not sin afterwards." As if he had ever heard anything of his subsequent perfection in righteousness, except so far as the Church commends to our faith that even Adam was delivered by the mercy of the Lord Christ. "As to his posterity also," says he, "not only are they not more infirm than he, but they actually fulfilled more commandments than he ever did, since he neglected to fulfil one,"—this posterity which he sees so born (as Adam certainly was not made), not only incapable of commandment, which they do not at all understand, but hardly capable of sucking the breast, when they are hungry! Yet even these would He have to be saved in the bosom of Mother Church by His grace who saves His people from their sins; but these men gainsay such grace, and, as if they had a deeper insight into the creature than ever He possesses who made the creature, they pronounce [these infants] sound with an assertion which is anything but sound itself.

Chapter 24 [XXII.]—Sin and the Penalty of Sin the Same.

"The very matter," says he, "of sin is its punishment, if the sinner is so much weakened that he commits more sins." He does not consider how justly the light of truth forsakes the man who transgresses the law. When thus deserted he of course becomes blinded, and necessarily offends more; and by so falling is embarrassed and being embarrassed fails to rise, so as to hear the voice of the law, which admonishes him to beg for the Savior's grace. Is no punishment due to them of whom the apostle says: "Because that, when they knew God, they glorified Him not as God, neither were thankful; but became vain in their imaginations, and their foolish heart was darkened?" This darkening was, of course, already their punishment and penalty; and yet by this very penalty—that is, by their blindness of heart, which supervenes on the withdrawal of the light of wisdom—they fell into more grievous sins still. "For giving themselves out as wise, they became fools." This is a grievous penalty, if one only understands it; and from such a penalty only see to what lengths they ran: "And they changed," he says, "the glory of the incorruptible God into an image made like to corruptible man, and to birds, and four-footed beasts, and creeping things." All this they did owing to that penalty of their sin, whereby "their foolish heart was darkened." And yet, owing to these deeds of theirs, which, although coming in the way of punishment, were none the less sins (he goes on to say): "Wherefore God also gave them up to uncleanness, through the lusts of their own hearts." See how severely God condemned them, giving them over to uncleanness in the very desires of their heart. Observe also the sins they commit owing to such condemnation: "To dishonor," says he, "their own bodies among themselves." Here is the punishment of iniquity, which is itself iniquity; a fact which sets forth in a clearer light the words which follow: "Who changed the truth of God into a lie, and worshipped and served the creature more than the Creator, who is blessed forever. Amen." "For this cause," says he, "God gave them up unto vile affections." See how often God inflicts punishment; and out of the self-same punishment sins, more numerous and more severe, arise. "For even their women did change the natural use into that which is against nature; and likewise the men also, leaving the natural use of the woman, burned in their lust one toward another; men with men working that which is unseemly." Then, to show that these things were so sins themselves, that they were also the penalties of sins, he further says: "And receiving in themselves that recompense of their error which was meet." Observe how often it happens that the very punishment which God inflicts begets other sins as its natural offspring. Attend still further: "And even as they did not like to retain God in their knowledge," says he, "God gave them over to a reprobate mind, to do those things which are not convenient; being filled with all unrighteousness, fornication, wickedness, covetousness, maliciousness; full of envy, murder, debate, deceit, malignity; whisperers, backbiters, odious to God, despiteful, proud, boasters, inventors of evil things, disobedient to parents, without understanding, covenant-breakers, without natural affection, implacable, unmerciful." Here, now, let our opponent say: "Sin ought not so to have been punished, that the sinner, through his punishment, should commit even more sins."

Chapter 25 [XXIII.]—God Forsakes Only Those Who Deserve to Be Forsaken. We are Sufficient of Ourselves to Commit Sin; But Not to Return to the Way of Righteousness. Death is the Punishment, Not the Cause of Sin.

Perhaps he may answer that God does not compel men to do these things, but only forsakes those who deserve to be forsaken. If he does say this, he says what is most true. For, as I have already remarked, those who are forsaken by the light of righteousness, and are therefore groping in darkness, produce nothing else than those works of darkness which I have enumerated, until such time as it is said to them, and they obey the command: "Awake thou that sleeps, and arise from the dead, and Christ shall give thee light." The truth designates them as dead; whence the passage: "Let the dead bury their dead." The truth, then, designates as dead those whom this man declares to have been unable to be damaged or corrupted by sin, on the ground, forsooth, that he has discovered sin to be no substance! Nobody tells him that "man was so formed as to be able to pass from righteousness to sin, and yet not able to return from sin to righteousness." But that free will, whereby man corrupted his own self, was sufficient for his passing into sin; but to return to righteousness, he has need of a Physician, since he is out of health; he has need of a Vivifier, because he is dead. Now about such grace as this he says not a word, as if he were able to cure himself by his own will, since this alone was able to ruin him. We do not tell him that the death of the body is of efficacy for sinning, because it is only its punishment; for no one sins by undergoing the death of his body; but the death of the soul is conducive to sin, forsaken as it is by its life, that is, its God; and it must needs produce dead works, until it revives by the grace of Christ. God forbid that we should assert that hunger and thirst and other bodily sufferings necessarily produce sin. When exercised by such vexations, the life of the righteous only shines out with greater luster, and procures a greater glory by overcoming them through patience; but then it is assisted by the grace, it is assisted by the Spirit, it is assisted by the mercy of God; not exalting itself in an arrogant will, but earning fortitude by a humble confession. For it had learnt to say unto God: "Thou art my hope; Thou art my trust." Now, how it happens that concerning this grace, and help and mercy, without which we cannot live, this man has nothing to say, I am at a loss to know; but he goes further, and in the most open manner gainsays the grace of Christ whereby we are justified, by insisting on the sufficiency of nature to work righteousness, provided only the will be present. The reason, however, why, after sin has been released to the guilty one by grace, for the exercise of faith, there should still remain the death of the body, although it proceeds from sin, I have already explained, according to my ability, in those books which I wrote to Marcellinus of blessed memory.

Chapter 26 [XXIV.]—Christ Died of His Own Power and Choice.

As to his statement, indeed, that "the Lord was able to die without sin;" His being born also was of the ability of His mercy, not the demand of His nature: so, likewise, did He undergo death of His own power; and this is our price which He paid to redeem us from death. Now, this truth their contention labors hard to make of none effect; for human nature is maintained by them to be such, that with free will it wants no such ransom in order to be translated from the power of darkness and of him who has the power of death, into the kingdom of Christ the Lord. And yet, when the Lord drew near His passion, He said, "Behold, the prince of this world cometh and shall find nothing in me,"—and therefore no sin, of course, because which he might exercise dominion over Him, so as to destroy Him. "But," added He, "that the world may know that I do the will of my Father, arise, let us go hence;" as much as to say, I am going to die, not through the necessity of sin, but in voluntariness of obedience.

Chapter 27. —Even Evils, Through God's Mercy, are of Use.

He asserts that "no evil is the cause of anything good;" as if punishment, forsooth, were good, although thereby many have been reformed. There are, then, evils which are of use by the wondrous mercy of God. Did that man experience some good thing, when he said, "Thou didst hide Thy face from me, and I was troubled?" Certainly not; and yet this very trouble was to him in a certain manner a remedy against his pride. For he had said in his prosperity, "I shall never be moved;" and so was ascribing to himself what he was receiving from the Lord. "For what had he that he did not receive?" It had, therefore, become necessary to show him whence he had received, that he might receive in humility what he had lost in pride. Accordingly, he says, "In Thy good pleasure, O Lord, Thou didst add strength to my beauty." In this abundance of mine I once used to say, "I shall not be moved;" whereas it all came from Thee, not from myself. Then at last Thou didst turn away Thy face from me, and I became troubled.

Chapter 28 [XXV.]—The Disposition of Nearly All Who Go Astray. With Some Heretics Our Business Ought Not to Be Disputation, But Prayer.

Man's proud mind has no relish at all for this; God, however, is great, in persuading even it how to find it all out. We are, indeed, more inclined to seek how best to reply to such arguments as oppose our error, than to experience how salutary would be our condition if we were free from error. We ought, therefore, to encounter all such, not by discussions, but rather by prayers both for them and for ourselves. For we never say to them, what this opponent has opposed to himself, that "sin was necessary in order that there might be a cause for God's mercy." Would there had never been misery to render that mercy necessary! But the iniquity of sin, —which is so much the greater in proportion to the ease wherewith man might have avoided sin, whilst no infirmity did as yet beset him, —has been followed closely up by a most righteous punishment; even that [offending man] should receive in himself a reward in kind of his sin, losing that obedience of his body which had been in some degree put under his own control, which he had despised when it was the right of his Lord. And, inasmuch as we are now born with the self-same law of sin, which in our members resists the law of our mind, we ought never to murmur against God, nor to dispute in opposition to the clearest fact, but to seek and pray for His mercy instead of our punishment.

Chapter 29 [XXVI.]—A Simile to Show that God's Grace is Necessary for Doing Any Good Work Whatever. God Never Forsakes the Justified Man If He Be Not Himself Forsaken.

Observe, indeed, how cautiously he expresses himself: "God, no doubt, applies His mercy even to this office, whenever it is necessary because man after sin requires help in this way, not because God wished there should be a cause for such necessity." Do you not see how he does not say that God's grace is necessary to prevent us from sinning, but because we have sinned? Then he adds: "But just in the same way it is the duty of a physician to be ready to cure a man who is already wounded; although he ought not to wish for a man who is sound to be wounded." Now, if this simile suits the subject of which we are treating, human nature is certainly incapable of receiving a wound from sin, inasmuch as sin is not a substance. As therefore, for example's sake, a man who is lamed by a wound is cured in order that his step for the future may be direct and strong, its past infirmity being healed, so does the Heavenly Physician cure our maladies, not only that they may cease any longer to exist, but in order that we may ever afterwards be able to walk aright, —to which we should be unequal, even after our healing, except by His continued help. For after a medical man has administered a cure, in order that the patient may be afterwards duly nourished with bodily elements and ailments, for the completion and continuance of the said cure by suitable means and help, he commends him to God's good care, who bestows these aids on all who live in the flesh, and from whom proceeded even those means which [the physician] applied during the process of the cure. For it is not out of any resources which he has himself created that the medical man effects any cure, but out of the resources of Him who creates all things which are required by the whole and by the sick. God, however, whenever He— through "the one mediator between God and men, the man Christ Jesus"—spiritually heals the sick or raises the dead, that is, justifies the ungodly, and when He has brought him to perfect health, in other words, to the fulness of life and righteousness, does not forsake, if He is not forsaken, in order that life may be passed in constant piety and righteousness. For, just as the eye of the body, even when completely sound, is unable to see unless aided by the brightness of light, so also man, even when most fully justified, is unable to lead a holy life, if he be not divinely assisted by the eternal light of righteousness. God, therefore, heals us not only that He may blot out the sin which we have committed, but, furthermore, that He may enable us even to avoid sinning.

Chapter 30 [XXVII.]—Sin is Removed by Sin.

He no doubt shows some acuteness in handling, and turning over and exposing, as he likes, and refuting a certain statement, which is made to this effect, that "it was really necessary to man, in order to take from him all occasion for pride and boasting, that he should be unable to exist without sin." He supposes it to be "the height of absurdity and folly, that there should have been sin in order that sin might not be; inasmuch as pride is itself, of course, a sin." As if a sore were not attended with pain, and an operation did not produce pain, that pain might be taken away by pain. If we had not experienced any such treatment, but were only to hear about it in some parts of the world where these things had never happened, we might perhaps use this man's words, and say, It is the height of absurdity that pain should have been necessary in order that a sore should have no pain.

Chapter 31.—The Order and Process of Healing Our Heavenly Physician Does Not Adopt from the Sick Patient, But Derives from Himself. What Cause the Righteous Have for Fearing.

"But God," they say, "is able to heal all things." Of course His purpose in acting is to heal all things; but He acts on His own judgment, and does not take His procedure in healing from the sick man. For undoubtedly it was His wish to endow His apostle with very great power and strength, and yet He said to him: "My strength is made perfect in weakness;" nor did He remove from him, though he so often entreated Him to do so, that mysterious "thorn in the flesh," which He told him had been given to him "lest he should be unduly exalted through the abundance of the revelation." For all other sins only prevail in evil deeds; pride only has to be guarded against in things that are rightly done. Whence it happens that those persons are admonished not to attribute to their own power the gifts of God, nor to plume themselves thereon, lest by so doing they should perish with a heavier perdition than if they had done no good at all, to whom it is said: "Work out your own salvation with fear and trembling, for it is God which worketh in you, both to will and to do of His good pleasure." Why, then, must it be with fear and trembling, and not rather with security, since God is working; except it be because there so quickly steals over our human soul, because of our will (without which we can do nothing well), the inclination to esteem simply as our own accomplishment whatever good we do; and so each one of us says in his prosperity: "I shall never be moved?" Therefore, He who in His good pleasure had added strength to our beauty, turns away His face, and the man who had made his boast becomes troubled, because it is by actual sorrows that the swelling pride must be remedied.

Chapter 32 [XXVIII.]—God Forsakes Us to Some Extent that We May Not Grow Proud.

Therefore it is not said to a man: "It necessary for you to sin that you may not sin;" but it is said to a man: "God in some degree forsakes you, in consequence of which you grow proud, that you may know that you are 'not your own,' but are His, and learn not to be proud."

Now even that incident in the apostle's life, of this kind, is so wonderful, that were it not for the fact that he himself is the voucher for it whose truth it is impious to contradict, would it not be incredible? For what believer is there who is ignorant that the first incentive to sin came from Satan, and that he is the first author of all sins? And yet, for all that, some are "delivered over unto Satan, that they may learn not to blaspheme." How comes it to pass, then, that Satan's work is prevented by the work of Satan? These and such like questions let a man regard in such a light that they seem not to him to be too acute; they have somewhat of the sound of acuteness, and yet when discussed are found to be obtuse. What must we say also to our author's use of similes whereby he rather suggests to us the answer which we should give to him? "What" (asks he) "shall I say more than this, that we may believe that fires are quenched by fires, if we may believe that sins are cured by sins?" What if one cannot put out fires by fires: but yet pains can, for all that, as I have shown, be cured by pains? Poisons can also, if one only inquire and learn the fact, be expelled by poisons. Now, if he observes that the heats of fevers are sometimes subdued by certain medicinal warmth, he will perhaps also allow that fires may be extinguished by fires.

Chapter 33 [XXIX.]—Not Every Sin is Pride. How Pride is the Commencement of Every Sin.

"But how," asks he, "shall we separate pride itself from sin?" Now, why does he raise such a question, when it is manifest that even pride itself is a sin? "To sin," says he, "is quite as much to be proud, as to be proud is to sin; for only ask what every sin is, and see whether you can find any sin without the designation of pride." Then he thus pursues this opinion, and endeavors to prove it thus: "Every sin," says he, "if I mistake not, is a contempt of God, and every contempt of God is pride. For what is so proud as to despise God? All sin, then, is also pride, even as Scripture says, Pride is the beginning of all sin." Let him seek diligently, and he will find in the law that the sin of pride is quite distinguished from all other sins. For many sins are committed through pride; but yet not all things which are wrongly done are done proudly, —at any rate, not by the ignorant, not by the infirm, and not, generally speaking, by the weeping and sorrowful. And indeed pride, although it be in itself a great sin, is of such sort in itself alone apart from others, that, as I have already remarked, it for the most part follows after and steals with more rapid foot, not so much upon sins as upon things which are actually well done. However, that which he has understood in another sense, is after all most truly said: "Pride is the commencement of all sin;" because it was this which overthrew the devil, from whom arose the origin of sin; and afterwards, when his malice and envy pursued man, who was yet standing in his uprightness, it subverted him in the same way in which he himself fell. For the serpent, in fact, only sought for the door of pride whereby to enter when he said, "Ye shall be as gods." Truly then is it said, "Pride is the commencement of all sin;" and, "The beginning of pride is when a man departed from God."

Chapter 34 [XXX.]—A Man's Sin is His Own, But He Needs Grace for His Cure.

Well, but what does he mean when he says: "Then again, how can one be subjected to God for the guilt of that sin, which he knows is not his own? For," says he, "his own it is not, if it is necessary. Or, if it is his own, it is voluntary: and if it is voluntary, it can be avoided." We reply: It is unquestionably his own. But the fault by which sin is committed is not yet in every respect healed, and the fact of its becoming permanently fixed in us arises from our not rightly using the healing virtue; and so out of this faulty condition the man who is now growing strong in depravity commits many sins, either through infirmity or blindness. Prayer must therefore be made for him, that he may be healed, and that he may thenceforward attain to a life of uninterrupted soundness of health; nor must pride be indulged in, as if any man were healed by the self-same power whereby he became corrupted.

Chapter 35 [XXXI.]—Why God Does Not Immediately Cure Pride Itself. The Secret and Insidious Growth of Pride. Preventing and Subsequent Grace.

But I would indeed so treat these topics, as to confess myself ignorant of God's deeper counsel, why He does not at once heal the very principle of pride, which lies in wait for man's heart even in deeds rightly done; and for the cure of which pious souls, with tears and strong crying, beseech Him that He would stretch forth His right hand and help their endeavors to overcome it, and somehow tread and crush it under foot. Now when a man has felt glad that he has even by some good work overcome pride, from the very joy he lifts up his head and says: "Behold, I live; why do you triumph? Nay, I live because you triumph." Premature, however, this forwardness of his to triumph over pride may perhaps be, as if it were now vanquished, whereas its last shadow is to be swallowed up, as I suppose, in that noontide which is promised in the scripture which says, "He shall bring forth thy righteousness as the light, and thy judgment as the noonday;" provided that be done which was written in the preceding verse: "Commit thy way unto the Lord; trust also in Him, and He shall bring it to pass,"—not, as some suppose, that they themselves bring it to pass. Now, when he said, "And He shall bring it to pass," he evidently had none other in mind but those who say, We ourselves bring it to pass; that is to say, we ourselves justify our own selves. In this matter, no doubt, we do ourselves, too, work; but we are fellow-workers with Him who does the work, because His mercy anticipates us. He anticipates us, however, that we may be healed; but then He will also follow us, that being healed we may grow healthy and strong. He anticipates us that we may be called; He will follow us that we may be glorified. He anticipates us that we may lead godly lives; He will follow us that we may always live with Him, because without Him we can do nothing. Now the Scriptures refer to both these operations of grace. There is both this: "The God of my mercy shall anticipate me," and again this: "Thy mercy shall follow me all the days of my life." Let us therefore unveil to Him our life by confession, not praise it with a vindication. For if it is not His way, but our own, beyond doubt it is not the right one. Let us therefore reveal this by making our confession to Him; for however much we may endeavor to conceal it, it is not hid from Him. It is a good thing to confess unto the Lord.

Chapter 36 [XXXII.]—Pride Even in Such Things as are Done Aright Must Be Avoided. Free Will is Not Taken Away When Grace is Preached.

So will He bestow on us whatever pleases Him, that if there be anything displeasing to Him in us, it will also be displeasing to us. "He will," as the Scripture has said, "turn aside our paths from His own way," and will make that which is His own to be our way; because it is by Himself that the favor is bestowed on such as believe in Him and hope in Him that we will do it. For there is a way of righteousness of which they are ignorant "who have a zeal for God, but not according to knowledge," and who, wishing to frame a righteousness of their own, "have not submitted themselves to the righteousness of God." "For Christ is the end of the law for righteousness to everyone that believeth;" and He has said, "I am the way." Yet God's voice has alarmed those who have already begun to walk in this way, lest they should be lifted up, as if it were by their own energies that they were walking therein. For the same persons to whom the apostle, because this danger, says, "Work out your own salvation with fear and trembling, for it is God that worketh in you, both to will and to do of His good pleasure," are likewise for the self-same reason admonished in the psalm: "Serve the Lord with fear, and rejoice in Him with trembling. Accept correction, lest at any time the Lord be angry, and ye perish from the righteous way, when His wrath shall be suddenly kindled upon you." He does not say, "Lest at any time the Lord be angry and refuse to show you the righteous way," or, "refuse to lead you into the way of righteousness;" but even after you are walking therein, he was able so to terrify as to say, "Lest ye perish from the righteous way." Now, whence could this arise if not from pride, which (as I have so often said, and must repeat again and again) must be guarded against even in things which are rightly done, that is, in the very way of righteousness, lest a man, by regarding as his own that which is really God's, lose what is God's and be reduced merely to what is his own? Let us then carry out the concluding injunction of this same psalm, "Blessed are all they that trust in Him," so that He may Himself indeed effect and Himself show His own way in us, to whom it is said, "Show us Thy mercy, O Lord;" and Himself bestow on us the pathway of safety that we may walk therein, to whom the prayer is offered, "And grant us Thy salvation;" and Himself lead us in the self-same way, to whom again it is said, "Guide me, O Lord, in Thy way, and in Thy truth will I walk;" Himself, too, conduct us to those promises whither His way leads, to whom it is said, "Even there shall Thy hand lead me and Thy right hand shall hold me;" Himself pasture therein those who sit down with Abraham, Isaac, and Jacob, of whom it is said, "He shall make them sit down to meat, and will come forth and serve them." Now we do not, when we make mention of these things, take away freedom of will, but we preach the grace of God. For to whom are those gracious gifts of use, but to the man who uses, but humbly uses, his own will, and makes no boast of the power and energy thereof, as if it alone were sufficient for perfecting him in righteousness?

Chapter 37 [XXXIII.]—Being Wholly Without Sin Does Not Put Man on an Equality with God.

But God forbid that we should meet him with such an assertion as he says certain persons advance against him: "That man is placed on an equality with God, if he is described as being without sin;" as if indeed an angel, because he is without sin, is put in such an equality. For my own part, I am of this opinion that the creature will never become equal with God, even when so perfect a holiness shall be accomplished in us, that it shall be quite incapable of receiving any addition. No; all who maintain that our progress is to be so complete that we shall be changed into the substance of God, and that we shall thus become what He is, should look well to it how they build up their opinion; for myself I must confess that I am not persuaded of this.

Chapter 38 [XXXIV.]—We Must Not Lie, Even for the Sake of Moderation. The Praise of Humility Must Not Be Placed to the Account of Falsehood.

I am favorably disposed, indeed, to the view of our author, when he resists those who say to him, "What you assert seems indeed to be reasonable, but it is an arrogant thing to allege that any man can be without sin," with this answer, that if it is at all true, it must not on any account be called an arrogant statement; for with very great truth and acuteness he asks, "On what side must humility be placed? No doubt on the side of falsehood, if you prove arrogance to exist on the side of truth." And so he decides, and rightly decides, that humility should rather be ranged on the side of truth, not of falsehood.

Whence it follows that he who said, "If we say that we have no sin, we deceive ourselves, and the truth is not in us," must without hesitation be held to have spoken the truth, and not be thought to have spoken falsehood for the sake of humility. Therefore, he added the words, "And the truth is not in us;" whereas it might perhaps have been enough if he merely said, "We deceive ourselves," if he had not observed that some can suppose that the clause "we deceive ourselves" is here employed because the man who praises himself is even extolled for a really good action. So that, by the addition of "the truth is not in us," he clearly shows (even as our author most correctly observes) that it is not at all true if we say that we have no sin, lest humility, if placed on the side of falsehood, should lose the reward of truth.

Chapter 39. —Pelagius Glorifies God as Creator at the Expense of God as Savior.

Beyond this, however, although he flatters himself that he vindicates the cause of God by defending nature, he forgets that by predicating soundness of the said nature, he rejects the Physician's mercy. He, however, who created him is also his Savior. We ought not, therefore, so to magnify the Creator as to be compelled to say, nay, rather as to be convicted of saying, that the Savior is superfluous. Man's nature indeed we may honor with worthy praise, and attribute the praise to the Creator's glory; but at the same time, while we show our gratitude to Him for having created us, let us not be ungrateful to Him for healing us. Our sins which He heals we must undoubtedly attribute not to God's operation, but to the willfulness of man, and submit them to His righteous punishment; as, however, we acknowledge that it was in our power that they should not be committed, so let us confess that it lies in His mercy rather than in our own power that they should be healed. But this mercy and remedial help of the Savior, according to this writer, consists only in this, that He forgives the transgressions that are past, not that He helps us to avoid such as are to come. Here he is most fatally mistaken; here, however unwittingly—here he hinders us from being watchful, and from praying that "we enter not into temptation," since he maintains that it lies entirely in our own control that this should not happen to us.

Chapter 40 [XXXV.]—Why There is a Record in Scripture of Certain Men's Sins, Recklessness in Sin Accounts It to Be So Much Loss Whenever It Falls Short in Gratifying Lust.

He who has a sound judgment says soundly, "that the examples of certain persons, of whose sinning we read in Scripture, are not recorded for this purpose, that they may encourage despair of not sinning, and seem somehow to afford security in committing sin,"—but that we may learn the humility of repentance, or else discover that even in such falls salvation ought not to be despaired of. For there are some who, when they have fallen into sin, perish rather from the recklessness of despair, and not only neglect the remedy of repentance, but become the slaves of lusts and wicked desires, so far as to run all lengths in gratifying these depraved and abandoned dispositions, —as if it were a loss to them if they failed to accomplish what their lust impelled them to, whereas all the while there awaits them a certain condemnation. To oppose this morbid recklessness, which is only too full of danger and ruin, there is great force in the record of those sins into which even just and holy men have before now fallen.

Chapter 41. —Whether Holy Men Have Died Without Sin.

But there is clearly much acuteness in the question put by our author, "How must we suppose that those holy men quitted this life, —with sin, or without sin?" For if we answer, "With sin," condemnation will be supposed to have been their destiny, which it is shocking to imagine; but if it be said that they departed this life "without sin," then it would be a proof that man had been without sin in his present life, at all events, when death was approaching. But, with all his acuteness, he overlooks the circumstance that even righteous persons not without good reason offer up this prayer: "Forgive us our debts, as we forgive our debtors;" and that the Lord Christ, after explaining the prayer in His teaching, most truly added: "For if ye forgive men their trespasses, your Father will also forgive you your trespasses." Here, indeed, we have the daily incense, so to speak, of the Spirit, which is offered to God on the altar of the heart, which we are bidden "to lift up,"—implying that, even if we cannot live here without sin, we may yet die without sin, when in merciful forgiveness the sin is blotted out which is committed in ignorance or infirmity.

Chapter 42 [XXXVI.]—The Blessed Virgin Mary May Have Lived Without Sin. None of the Saints Besides Her Without Sin.

He then enumerates those "who not only lived without sin, but are described as having led holy lives, — Abel, Enoch, Melchizedek, Abraham, Isaac, Jacob, Joshua the son of Nun, Phinehas, Samuel, Nathan, Elijah, Joseph, Elisha, Micaiah, Daniel, Hananiah, Azariah, Mishael, Mordecai, Simeon, Joseph to whom the Virgin Mary was espoused, John." And he adds the names of some women, — "Deborah, Anna the mother of Samuel, Judith, Esther, the other Anna, daughter of Phanuel, Elisabeth, and also the mother of our Lord and Savior, for of her," he says, "we must needs allow that her piety had no sin in it." We must except the holy Virgin Mary, concerning whom I wish to raise no question when it touches the subject of sins, out of honor to the Lord; for from Him we know what abundance of grace for overcoming sin in every particular was conferred upon her who had the merit to conceive and bear Him who undoubtedly had no sin. Well, then, if, with this exception of the Virgin, we could only assemble together all the aforementioned holy men and women, and ask them whether they lived without sin whilst they were in this life, what can we suppose would be their answer? Would it be in the language of our author, or in the words of the Apostle John? I put it to you, whether, on having such a question submitted to them, however excellent might have been their sanctity in this body, they would not have exclaimed with one voice: "If we say we have no sin, we deceive ourselves, and the truth is not in us?" But perhaps this their answer would have been more humble than true!

Well, but our author has already determined, and rightly determined, "not to place the praise of humility on the side of falsehood." If, therefore, they spoke the truth in giving such an answer, they would have sin, and since they humbly acknowledged it, the truth would be in them; but if they lied in their answer, they would still have sin, because the truth would not be in them.

Chapter 43 [XXXVII.]—Why Scripture Has Not Mentioned the Sins of All.

"But perhaps," says he, "they will ask me: Could not the Scripture have mentioned sins of all of these?" And surely they would say the truth, whoever should put such a question to him; and I do not discover that he has anywhere given a sound reply to them, although I perceive that he was unwilling to be silent. What he has said, I beg of you to observe: "This," says he, "might be rightly asked of those whom Scripture mentions neither as good nor as bad; but of those whose holiness it commemorates, it would also without doubt have commemorated the sins likewise, if it had perceived that they had sinned in anything." Let him say, then, that their great faith did not attain to righteousness in the case of those who comprised "the multitudes that went before and that followed" the colt on which the Lord rode, when "they shouted and said, Hosanna to the Son of David: Blessed is He that cometh in the name of the Lord," even amidst the malignant men who with murmurs asked why they were doing all this! Let him then boldly tell us, if he can, that there was not a man in all that vast crowd who had any sin at all. Now, if it is most absurd to make such a statement as this, why has not the Scripture mentioned any sins in the persons to whom reference has been made, especially when it has carefully recorded the eminent goodness of their faith?

Chapter 44. —Pelagius Argues that Abel Was Sinless.

This, however, even he probably observed, and therefore he went on to say: "But, granted that it has sometimes abstained, in a numerous crowd, from narrating the sins of all; still, in the very beginning of the world, when there were only four persons in existence, what reason (asks he) have we to give why it chose not to mention the sins of all? Was it in consideration of the vast multitude, which had not yet come into existence? or because, having mentioned only the sins of those who had transgressed, it was unable to record any of him who had not yet committed sin?" And then he proceeds to add some words, in which he unfolds this idea with a fuller and more explicit illustration. "It is certain," says he, "that in the earliest age Adam and Eve, and Cain and Abel their sons, are mentioned as being the only four persons then in being. Eve sinned, —the Scripture distinctly says so much; Adam also transgressed, as the same Scripture does not fail to inform us; whilst it affords us an equally clear testimony that Cain also sinned: and of all these it not only mentions the sins, but also indicates the character of their sins. Now if Abel had likewise sinned, Scripture would without doubt have said so. But it has not said so, therefore he committed no sin; nay, it even shows him to have been righteous. What we read, therefore, let us believe; and what we do not read, let us deem it wicked to add."

Chapter 45 [XXXVIII.]—Why Cain Has Been by Some Thought to Have Had Children by His Mother Eve. The Sins of Righteous Men. Who Can Be Both Righteous, and Yet Not Without Sin.

When he says this, he forgets what he had himself said not long before: "After the human race had multiplied, it was possible that in the crowd the Scripture may have neglected to notice the sins of all men." If indeed he had borne this well in mind, he would have seen that even in one man there was such a crowd and so vast a number of slight sins, that it would have been impossible (or, even if possible, not desirable) to describe them. For only such are recorded as the due bounds allowed, and as would, by few examples, serve for instructing the reader in the many cases where he needed warning. Scripture has indeed omitted to mention concerning the few persons who were then in existence, either how many or who they were,—in other words, how many sons and daughters Adam and Eve begat, and what names they gave them; and from this circumstance some, not considering how many things are quietly passed over in Scripture, have gone so far as to suppose that Cain cohabited with his mother, and by her had the children which are mentioned, thinking that Adam's sons had no sisters, because Scripture failed to mention them in the particular place, although it afterwards, in the way of recapitulation, implied what it had previously omitted,— that "Adam begat sons and daughters," without, however, dropping a syllable to intimate either their number or the time when they were born. In like manner it was unnecessary to state whether Abel, notwithstanding that he is rightly styled "righteous," ever indulged in immoderate laughter, or was ever jocose in moments of relaxation, or ever looked at an object with a covetous eye, or ever plucked fruit to extravagance, or ever suffered indigestion from too much eating, or ever in the midst of his prayers permitted his thoughts to wander and call him away from the purpose of his devotion; as well as how frequently these and many other similar failings stealthily crept over his mind. And are not these failings sins, about which the apostle's precept gives us a general admonition that we should avoid and restrain them, when he says: "Let not sin therefore reign in your mortal body, that ye should obey it in the lusts thereof?" To escape from such an obedience, we must struggle in a constant and daily conflict against unlawful and unseemly inclinations. Only let the eye be directed, or rather abandoned, to an object which it ought to avoid, and let the mischief strengthen and get the mastery, and adultery is consummated in the body, which is committed in the heart only so much more quickly as thought is more rapid than action and there is no impediment to retard and delay it. They who in a great degree have curbed this sin, that is, this appetite of a corrupt affection, so as not to obey its desires, nor to "yield their members to it as instruments of unrighteousness," have fairly deserved to be called righteous persons, and this by the help of the grace of God. Since, however, sin often stole over them in very small matters, and when they were off their guard, they were both righteous, and at the same time not sinless. To conclude, if there was in righteous Abel that love of God whereby alone he is truly righteous who is righteous, to enable him, and to lay him under a moral obligation, to advance in holiness, still in whatever degree he fell short therein was of sin. And who indeed can help thus falling short, until he come to that mighty power thereof, in which man's entire infirmity shall be swallowed up?

Chapter 46 [XXXIX.]—Shall We Follow Scripture, or Add to Its Declarations?

It is, to be sure, a grand sentence with which he concluded this passage, when he says: "What we read, therefore, let us believe; and what we do not read, let us deem it wicked to add; and let it suffice to have said this of all cases." On the contrary, I for my part say that we ought not to believe even everything that we read, on the sanction of the apostle's advice: "Read all things; hold fast that which is good." Nor is it wicked to add something which we have not read; for it is in our power to add something which we have bona fide experienced as witnesses, even if it so happens that we have not read about it. Perhaps he will say in reply: "When I said this, I was treating of the Holy Scriptures." Oh how I wish that he were never willing to add, I will not say anything but what he reads in the Scriptures, but in opposition to what he reads in them; that he would only faithfully and obediently hear that which is written there: "By one man sin entered into the world, and death by sin, and so death passed upon all men; in which all have sinned;" and that he would not weaken the grace of the great Physician,— all by his unwillingness to confess that human nature is corrupted! Oh how I wish that he would, as a Christian, read the sentence, "There is none other name under heaven given among men whereby we must be saved;" and that he would not so uphold the possibility of human nature, as to believe that man can be saved by free will without that Name!

Chapter 47 [XL.]—For What Pelagius Thought that Christ is Necessary to Us.

Perhaps, however, he thinks the name of Christ to be necessary on this account, that by His gospel we may learn how we ought to live; but not that we may be also assisted by His grace, in order withal to lead good lives. Well, even this consideration should lead him at least to confess that there is a miserable darkness in the human mind, which knows how it ought to tame a lion, but knows not how to live. To know this, too, is it enough for us to have free will and natural law? This is that wisdom of word, whereby "the cross of Christ is rendered of none effect." He, however, who said, "I will destroy the wisdom of the wise," since that cross cannot be made of none effect, in very deed overthrows that wisdom by the foolishness of preaching whereby believers are healed. For if natural capacity, by help of free will, is in itself sufficient both for discovering how one ought to live, and also for leading a holy life, then "Christ died in vain," and therefore also "the offence of the cross is ceased." Why also may I not myself exclaim? —nay, I will exclaim, and chide them with a Christian's sorrow, — "Christ is become of no effect unto you, whosoever of you are justified by nature; ye are fallen from grace;" for, "being ignorant of God's righteousness, and wishing to establish your own righteousness, you have not submitted yourselves to the righteousness of God." For even as "Christ is the end of the law," so likewise is He the Savior of man's corrupted nature, "for righteousness to everyone that believeth."

Chapter 48 [XLI.]—How the Term "All" Is to Be Understood.

His opponents adduced the passage, "All have sinned," and he met their statement founded on this with the remark that "the apostle was manifestly speaking of the then existing generation, that is, the Jews and the Gentiles;" but surely the passage which I have quoted, "By one man sin entered the world, and death by sin, and so death passed upon all men; in which all have sinned," embraces in its terms the generations both of old and of modern times, both ourselves and our posterity. He adduces also this passage, whence he would prove that we ought not to understand all without exception, when "all" is used: — "As by the offence of one," he says, "upon all men to condemnation, even so by the righteousness of One, upon all men unto justification of life." "There can be no doubt," he says, "that not all men are sanctified by the righteousness of Christ, but only those who are willing to obey Him, and have been cleansed in the washing of His baptism." Well, but he does not prove what he wants by this quotation. For as the clause, "By the offence of one, upon all men to condemnation," is so worded that not one is omitted in its sense, so in the corresponding clause, "By the righteousness of One, upon all men unto justification of life," no one is omitted in its sense, —not, indeed, because all men have faith and are washed in His baptism, but because no man is justified unless he believes in Christ and is cleansed by His baptism. The term "all" is therefore used in a way which shows that no one whatever can be supposed able to be saved by any other means than through Christ Himself. For if in a city there be appointed but one instructor, we are most correct in saying: That man teaches all in that place; not meaning, indeed, that all who live in the city take lessons of him, but that no one is instructed unless taught by him. In like manner no one is justified unless Christ has justified him.

Chapter 49 [XLII.]—A Man Can Be Sinless, But Only by the Help of Grace. In the Saints This Possibility Advances and Keeps Pace with the Realization.

"Well, be it so," says he, "I agree; he testifies to the fact that all were sinners. He says, indeed, what they have been, not that they might not have been something else. Wherefore," he adds, "if all then could be proved to be sinners, it would not by any means prejudice our own definite position, in insisting not so much on what men are, as on what they are able to be." He is right for once to allow that no man living is justified in God's sight. He contends, however, that this is not the question, but that the point lies in the possibility of a man's not sinning,— on which subject it is unnecessary for us to take ground against him; for, in truth, I do not much care about expressing a definite opinion on the question, whether in the present life there ever have been, or now are, or ever can be, any persons who have had, or are having, or are to have, the love of God so perfectly as to admit of no addition to it (for nothing short of this amounts to a most true, full, and perfect righteousness). For I ought not too sharply to contend as to when, or where, or in whom is done that which I confess and maintain can be done by the will of man, aided by the grace of God. Nor do I indeed contend about the actual possibility, forasmuch as the possibility under dispute advances with the realization in the saints, their human will being healed and helped; whilst "the love of God," as fully as our healed and cleansed nature can possibly receive it, "is shed abroad in our hearts by the Holy Ghost, which is given to us." In a better way, therefore, is God's cause promoted (and it is to its promotion that our author professes to apply his warm defense of nature) when He is acknowledged as our Savior no less than as our Creator, than when His succor to us as Savior is impaired and dwarfed to nothing by the defense of the creature, as if it were sound and its resources entire.

Chapter 50 [XLIII.]—God Commands No Impossibilities.

What he says, however, is true enough, "that God is as good as just, and made man such that he was quite able to live without the evil of sin, if only he had been willing." For who does not know that man was made whole and faultless, and endowed with a free will and a free ability to lead a holy life? Our present inquiry, however, is about the man whom "the thieves" left half dead on the road, and who, being disabled and pierced through with heavy wounds, is not so able to mount up to the heights of righteousness as he was able to descend therefrom; who, moreover, if he is now in "the inn," is in process of cure. God therefore does not command impossibilities; but in His command He counsels you both to do what you can for yourself, and to ask His aid in what you cannot do. Now, we should see whence comes the possibility, and whence the impossibility. This man says: "That proceeds not from a man's will which he can do by nature." I say: A man is not righteous by his will if he can be by nature. He will, however, be able to accomplish by remedial aid what he is rendered incapable of doing by his flaw.

Chapter 51 [XLIV.]—State of the Question Between the Pelagians and the Catholics. Holy Men of Old Saved by the Self-Same Faith in Christ Which We Exercise.

But why need we tarry longer on general statements? Let us go into the core of the question, which we must discuss with our opponents solely, or almost entirely, on one particular point. For inasmuch as he says that "as far as the present question is concerned, it is not pertinent to inquire whether there have been or now are any men in this life without sin, but whether they had or have the ability to be such persons;" so, were I even to allow that there have been or are any such, I should not by any means therefore affirm that they had or have the ability, unless justified by the grace of God through our Lord "Jesus Christ and Him crucified." For the same faith which healed the saints of old now heals us, —that is to say, faith "in the one Mediator between God and men, the man Christ Jesus,"—faith in His blood, faith in His cross, faith in His death and resurrection. As we therefore have the same spirit of faith, we also believe, and on that account also speak.

Chapter 52. —The Whole Discussion is About Grace.

Let us, however, observe what our author answers, after laying before himself the question wherein he seems indeed so intolerable to Christian hearts. He says: "But you will tell me this is what disturbs a great many, —that you do not maintain that it is by the grace of God that a man is able to be without sin." Certainly, this is what causes us disturbance; this is what we object to him. He touches the very point of the case. This is what causes us such utter pain to endure it; this is why we cannot bear to have such points debated by Christians, owing to the love which we feel towards others and towards themselves. Well, let us hear how he clears himself from the objectionable character of the question he has raised. "What blindness of ignorance," he exclaims, "what sluggishness of an uninstructed mind, which supposes that that is maintained and held to be without God's grace which it only hears ought to be attributed to God!" Now, if we knew nothing of what follows this outburst of his, and formed our opinion on simply hearing these words, we might suppose that we had been led to a wrong view of our opponents by the spread of report and by the asseveration of some suitable witnesses among the brethren. For how could it have been more pointedly and truly stated that the possibility of not sinning, to whatever extent it exists or shall exist in man, ought only to be attributed to God? This too is our own affirmation. We may shake hands.

Chapter 53 [XLV.]—Pelagius Distinguishes Between a Power and Its Use.

Well, are there other things to listen to? Yes, certainly; both to listen to, and correct and guard against. "Now, when it is said," he says, "that the very ability is not at all of man's will, but of the Author of nature, —that is, God, —how can that possibly be understood to be without the grace of God which is deemed especially to belong to God?" Already we begin to see what he means; but that we may not lie under any mistake, he explains himself with greater breadth and clearness: "That this may become still plainer, we must," says he, "enter on a somewhat fuller discussion of the point. Now we affirm that the possibility of anything lies not so much in the ability of a man's will as in the necessity of nature." He then proceeds to illustrate his meaning by examples and similes. "Take," says he, "for instance, my ability to speak. That I can speak is not my own; but that I do speak is my own, —that is, of my own will. And because the act of my speaking is my own, I have the power of alternative action, —that is to say, both to speak and to refrain from speaking. But because my ability to speak is not my own, that is, is not of my own determination and will, it is of necessity that I am always able to speak; and though I wished not to be able to speak, I am unable, nevertheless, to be unable to speak, unless perhaps I were to deprive myself of that member whereby the function of speaking is to be performed." Many means, indeed, might be mentioned whereby, if he wish it, a man may deprive himself of the possibility of speaking, without removing the organ of speech. If, for instance, anything was to happen to a man to destroy his voice, he would be unable to speak, although the members remained; for a man's voice is of course no member. There may, in short, be an injury done to the member internally, short of the actual loss of it. I am, however, unwilling to press the argument for a word; and it may be replied to me in the contest, Why, even to injure is to lose. But yet we can so contrive matters, by closing and shutting the mouth with bandages, as to be quite incapable of opening it, and to put the opening of it out of our power, although it was quite in our own power to shut it while the strength and healthy exercise of the limbs remained.

Chapter 54 [XLVI.]—There is No Incompatibility Between Necessity and Free Will.

Now how does all this apply to our subject? Let us see what he makes out of it. "Whatever," says he, "is fettered by natural necessity is deprived of determination of will and deliberation." Well, now, here lies a question; for it is the height of absurdity for us to say that it does not belong to our will that we wish to be happy, because it is absolutely impossible for us to be unwilling to be happy, because of some indescribable but amiable coercion of our nature; nor dare we maintain that God has not the will but the necessity of righteousness, because He cannot will to sin.

Chapter 55 [XLVII.]—The Same Continued.

Mark also what follows. "We may perceive," says he, "the same thing to be true of hearing, smelling, and seeing, —that to hear, and to smell, and to see is of our own power, while the ability to hear, and to smell, and to see is not of our own power, but lies in a natural necessity." Either I do not understand what he means, or he does not himself. For how is the possibility of seeing not in our own power, if the necessity of not seeing is in our own power because blindness is in our own power, by which we can deprive ourselves, if we will, of this very ability to see? How, moreover, is it in our own power to see whenever we will, when, without any loss whatever to our natural structure of body in the organ of sight, we are unable, even though we wish, to see, —either by the removal of all external lights during the night, or by our being shut up in some dark place? Likewise, if our ability or our inability to hear is not in our own power, but lies in the necessity of nature, whereas our actual hearing or not hearing is of our own will, how comes it that he is inattentive to the fact that there are so many things which we hear against our will, which penetrate our sense even when our ears are stopped, as the creaking of a saw near to us, or the grunt of a pig? Although the said stopping of our ears shows plainly enough that it does not lie within our own power not to hear so long as our ears are open; perhaps, too, such a stopping of our ears as shall deprive us of the entire sense in question proves that even the ability not to hear lies within our own power. As to his remarks, again, concerning our sense of smell, does he not display no little carelessness when he says, "that it is not in our own power to be able or to be unable to smell, but that it is in our own power"—that is to say, in our free will— "to smell or not to smell?" For let us suppose someone to place us, with our hands firmly tied, but yet without any injury to our olfactory members, among some bad and noxious smells; in such a case we altogether lose the power, however strong may be our wish, not to smell, because every time we are obliged to draw breath we also inhale the smell which we do not wish.

Chapter 56 [XLVIII.]—The Assistance of Grace in a Perfect Nature.

Not only, then, are these similes employed by our author false, but so is the matter which he wishes them to illustrate. He goes on to say: "In like manner, touching the possibility of our not sinning, we must understand that it is of us not to sin, but yet that the ability to avoid sin is not of us." If he were speaking of man's whole and perfect nature, which we do not now possess ("for we are saved by hope: but hope that is seen is not hope. But if we hope for that we see not, then do we with patience wait for it"), his language even in that case would not be correct to the effect that to avoid sinning would be of us alone, although to sin would be of us, for even then there must be the help of God, which must shed itself on those who are willing to receive it, just as the light is given to strong and healthy eyes to assist them in their function of sight. Inasmuch, however, as it is about this present life of ours that he raises the question, wherein our corruptible body weighs down the soul, and our earthly tabernacle depresses our sense with all its many thoughts, I am astonished that he can with any heart suppose that, even without the help of our Savior's healing balm, it is in our own power to avoid sin, and the ability not to sin is of nature, which gives only stronger evidence of its own corruption by the very fact of its failing to see its taint.

Chapter 57 [XLIX.]—It Does Not Detract from God's Almighty Power, that He is Incapable of Either Sinning, or Dying, or Destroying Himself.

"Inasmuch," says he, "as not to sin is ours, we are able to sin and to avoid sin." What, then, if another should say: "Inasmuch as not to wish for unhappiness is ours, we are able both to wish for it and not to wish for it?" And yet we are positively unable to wish for it. For who could possibly wish to be unhappy, even though he wishes for something else from which unhappiness will ensue to him against his will? Then again, inasmuch as, in an infinitely greater degree, it is God's not to sin, shall we therefore venture to say that He is able both to sin and to avoid sin? God forbid that we should ever say that He is able to sin! For He cannot, as foolish persons suppose, therefore fail to be almighty, because He is unable to die, or because He cannot deny Himself. What, therefore, does he mean? by what method of speech does he try to persuade us on a point which he is himself loth to consider? For he advances a step further, and says: "Inasmuch as, however, it is not of us to be able to avoid sin; even if we were to wish not to be able to avoid sin, it is not in our power to be unable to avoid sin." It is an involved sentence, and therefore a very obscure one. It might, however, be more plainly expressed in some such way as this: "Inasmuch as to be able to avoid sin is not of us, then, whether we wish it or do not wish it, we are able to avoid sin!" He does not say, "Whether we wish it or do not wish it, we do not sin,"—for we undoubtedly do sin, if we wish; —but yet he asserts that, whether we will or not, we have the capacity of not sinning, —a capacity which he declares to be inherent in our nature. Of a man, indeed, who has his legs strong and sound, it may be said admissibly enough, "whether he will or not he has the capacity of walking;" but if his legs be broken, however much he may wish, he has not the capacity. The nature of which our author speaks is corrupted. "Why is dust and ashes proud?" It is corrupted. It implores the Physician's help. "Save me, O Lord," is its cry; "Heal my soul," it exclaims. Why does he check such cries so as to hinder future health, by insisting, as it were, on its present capacity?

Chapter 58 [L.]—Even Pious and God-Fearing Men Resist Grace.

Observe also what remark he adds, by which he thinks that his position is confirmed: "No will," says he, "can take away that which is proved to be inseparably implanted in nature." Whence then comes that utterance: "So then ye cannot do the things that ye would?" Whence also this: "For what good I would, that I do not; but what evil I hate, that do I?" Where is that capacity which is proved to be inseparably implanted in nature? See, it is human beings who do not what they will; and it is about not sinning, certainly, that he was treating, —not about not flying, because it was men not birds, that formed his subject. Behold, it is man who does not the good which he would, but does the evil which he would not: "to will is present with him, but how to perform that which is good is not present." Where is the capacity which is proved to be inseparably implanted in nature? For whomsoever the apostle represents by himself, if he does not speak these things of his own self, he certainly represents a man by himself. By our author, however, it is maintained that our human nature actually possesses an inseparable capacity of not at all sinning. Such a statement, however, even when made by a man who knows not the effect of his words (but this ignorance is hardly attributable to the man who suggests these statements for unwary though God-fearing men), causes the grace of Christ to be "made of none effect," since it is pretended that human nature is sufficient for its own holiness and justification.

Chapter 59 [LI.]—In What Sense Pelagius Attributed to God's Grace the Capacity of Not Sinning.

In order, however, to escape from the odium wherewith Christians guard their salvation, he parries their question when they ask him, "Why do you affirm that man without the help of God's grace is able to avoid sin?" by saying, "The actual capacity of not sinning lies not so much in the power of will as in the necessity of nature. Whatever is placed in the necessity of nature undoubtedly appertans to the Author of nature, that is, God. How then," says he, "can that be regarded as spoken without the grace of God which is shown to belong in an especial manner to God?" Here the opinion is expressed which all along was kept in the background; there is, in fact, no way of permanently concealing such a doctrine. The reason why he attributes to the grace of God the capacity of not sinning is, that God is the Author of nature, in which, he declares, this capacity of avoiding sin is inseparably implanted. Whenever He wills a thing, no doubt He does it; and what He wills not, that He does not. Now, wherever there is this inseparable capacity, there cannot accrue any infirmity of the will; or rather, there cannot be both a presence of will and a failure in "performance." This, then, being the case, how comes it to pass that "to will is present, but how to perform that which is good" is not present? Now, if the author of the work we are discussing spoke of that nature of man, which was in the beginning created faultless and perfect, in whatever sense his dictum be taken, "that it has an inseparable capacity,"—that is, so to say, one which cannot be lost,—then that nature ought not to have been mentioned at all which could be corrupted, and which could require a physician to cure the eyes of the blind, and restore that capacity of seeing which had been lost through blindness. For I suppose a blind man would like to see, but is unable; but, whenever a man wishes to do a thing and cannot, there is present to him the will, but he has lost the capacity.

Chapter 60 [LII.]—Pelagius Admits "Contrary Flesh" In the Unbaptized.

See what obstacles he still attempts to break through, if possible, in order to introduce his own opinion. He raises a question for himself in these terms: "But you will tell me that, according to the apostle, the flesh is contrary to us;" and then answers it in this wise: "How can it be that in the case of any baptized person the flesh is contrary to him, when according to the same apostle he is understood not to be in the flesh? For he says, 'But ye are not in the flesh.'" Very well; we shall soon see whether it be really true that this says that in the baptized the flesh cannot be contrary to them; at present, however, as it was impossible for him quite to forget that he was a Christian (although his reminiscence on the point is but slight), he has quitted his defense of nature. Where then is that inseparable capacity of his? Are those who are not yet baptized not a part of human nature? Well, now, here by all means, here at this point, he might find his opportunity of awaking out of his sleep; and he still has it if he is careful. "How can it be," he asks, "that in the case of a baptized person the flesh is contrary to him?" Therefore to the unbaptized the flesh can be contrary! Let him tell us how; for even in these there is that nature which has been so stoutly defended by him. However, in these he does certainly allow that nature is corrupted, inasmuch as it was only among the baptized that the wounded traveler left his inn sound and well, or rather remains sound in the inn whither the compassionate Samaritan carried him that he might become cured. Well, now, if he allows that the flesh is contrary even in these, let him tell us what has happened to occasion this, since the flesh and the spirit alike are the work of one and the same Creator, and are therefore undoubtedly both of them good, because He is good, —unless indeed it be that damage which has been inflicted by man's own will. And that this may be repaired in our nature, there is need of that very Savior from whose creative hand nature itself proceeded. Now, if we acknowledge that this Savior, and that healing remedy of His by which the Word was made flesh in order to dwell among us, are required by small and great, —by the crying infant and the hoary-headed man alike, —then, in fact, the whole controversy of the point between us is settled.

Chapter 61 [LIII.]—Paul Asserts that the Flesh is Contrary Even in the Baptized.

Now let us see whether we anywhere read about the flesh being contrary in the baptized also. And here, I ask, to whom did the apostle say, "The flesh lusted against the Spirit, and the Spirit against the flesh: and these are contrary the one to the other; so that ye do not the things that ye would?" He wrote this, I apprehend, to the Galatians, to whom he also says, "He therefore that ministered to you the Spirit, and worketh miracles among you, doeth he it by the works of the law or by the hearing of faith?" It appears, therefore, that it is to Christians that he speaks, to whom, too, God had given His Spirit: therefore, too, to the baptized. Observe, therefore, that even in baptized persons the flesh is found to be contrary; so that they have not that capacity which, our author says, is inseparably implanted in nature. Where then is the ground for his assertion, "How can it be that in the case of a baptized person the flesh is contrary to him?" in whatever sense he understands the flesh? Because in very deed it is not its nature that is good, but it is the carnal defects of the flesh which are expressly named in the passage before us. Yet observe, even in the baptized, how contrary is the flesh. And in what way contrary? So that, "They do not the things which they would." Take notice that the will is present in a man; but where is that "capacity of nature?" Let us confess that grace is necessary to us; let us cry out, "O wretched man that I am! who shall deliver me from the body of this death?" And let our answer be, "The grace of God, through Jesus Christ our Lord!"

Chapter 62. —Concerning What Grace of God is Here Under Discussion. The Ungodly Man, When Dying, is Not Delivered from Concupiscence.

Now, whereas it is most correctly asked in those words put to him, "Why do you affirm that man without the help of God's grace is able to avoid sin?" yet the inquiry did not concern that grace by which man was created, but only that whereby he is saved through Jesus Christ our Lord. Faithful men say in their prayer, "Lead us not into temptation, but deliver us from evil." But if they already have capacity, why do they pray? Or, what is the evil which they pray to be delivered from, but, above all else, "the body of this death?" And from this nothing but God's grace alone delivers them, through our Lord Jesus Christ. Not of course from the substance of the body, which is good; but from its carnal offences, from which a man is not liberated except by the grace of the Savior, —not even when he quits the body by the death of the body. If it was this that the apostle meant to declare, why had he previously said, "I see another law in my members, warring against the law of my mind, and bringing me into captivity to the law of sin which is in my members?" Behold what damage the disobedience of the will has inflicted on man's nature! Let him be permitted to pray that he may be healed! Why need he presume so much on the capacity of his nature? It is wounded, hurt, damaged, destroyed. It is a true confession of its weakness, not a false defense of its capacity, that it stands in need of. It requires the grace of God, not that it may be made, but that it may be re-made. And this is the only grace which by our author is proclaimed to be unnecessary; because of this he is silent! If, indeed, he had said nothing at all about God's grace, and had not proposed to himself that question for solution, for the purpose of removing from himself the odium of this matter, it might have been thought that his view of the subject was consistent with the truth, only that he had refrained from mentioning it, because not on all occasions need we say all we think. He proposed the question of grace, and answered it in the way that he had in his heart; the question has been defined, —not in the way we wished, but according to the doubt we entertained as to what was his meaning.

Chapter 63 [LIV.]—Does God Create Contraries?

He next endeavors, by much quotation from the apostle, about which there is no controversy, to show "that the flesh is often mentioned by him in such a manner as proves him to mean not the substance, but the works of the flesh." What is this to the point? The defects of the flesh are contrary to the will of man; his nature is not accused; but a Physician is wanted for its defects. What signifies his question, "Who made man's spirit?" and his own answer thereto, "God, without a doubt?" Again he asks, "Who created the flesh?" and again answers, "The same God, I suppose." And yet a third question, "Is the God good who created both?" and the third answer, "Nobody doubts it." Once more a question, "Are not both good, since the good Creator made them?" and its answer, "It must be confessed that they are." And then follows his conclusion: "If, therefore, both the spirit is good, and the flesh is good, as made by the good Creator, how can it be that the two good things should be contrary to one another?" I need not say that the whole of this reasoning would be upset if one were to ask him, "Who made heat and cold?" and he were to say in answer, "God, without a doubt." I do not ask the string of questions. Let him determine himself whether these conditions of climate may either be said to be not good, or else whether they do not seem to be contrary to each other. Here he will probably object, "These are not substances, but the qualities of substances." Very true, it is so. But still they are natural qualities, and undoubtedly belong to God's creation; and substances, indeed, are not said to be contrary to each other in themselves, but in their qualities, as water and fire. What if it be so too with flesh and spirit? We do not affirm it to be so; but, in order to show that his argument terminates in a conclusion which does not necessarily follow, we have said so much as this. For it is quite possible for contraries not to be reciprocally opposed to each other, but rather by mutual action to temper health and render it good; just as, in our body, dryness and moisture, cold and heat, —in the tempering of which altogether consists our bodily health. The fact, however, that "the flesh is contrary to the Spirit, so that we cannot do the things that we would," is a defect, not nature. The Physician's grace must be sought, and their controversy must end.

Chapter 64. —Pelagius' Admission as Regards the Unbaptized, Fatal.

Now, as touching these two good substances which the good God created, how, against the reasoning of this man, in the case of unbaptized persons, can they be contrary the one to the other? Will he be sorry to have said this too, which he admitted out of some regard to the

Christians' faith? For when he asked, "How, in the case of any person who is already baptized, can it be that his flesh is contrary to him?" he intimated, of course, that in the case of unbaptized persons it is possible for the flesh to be contrary. For why insert the clause, "who is already baptized," when without such an addition he might have put his question thus: "How in the case of any person can the flesh be contrary?" and when, in order to prove this, he might have subjoined that argument of his, that as both body and spirit are good (made as they are by the good Creator), they therefore cannot be contrary to each other? Now, suppose unbaptized persons (in whom, at any rate, he confesses that the flesh is contrary) were to ply him with his own arguments, and say to him, Who made man's spirit? he must answer, God. Suppose they asked him again, Who created the flesh? and he answers, The same God, I believe. Suppose their third question to be, Is the God good who created both? and his reply to be, Nobody doubts it. Suppose once more they put to him his yet remaining inquiry, Are not both good, since the good Creator made them? and he confesses it. Then surely, they will cut his throat with his own sword, when they force home his conclusion on him, and say: Since therefore the spirit of man is good, and his flesh good, as made by the good Creator, how can it be that the two being good should be contrary to one another? Here, perhaps, he will reply: I beg your pardon, I ought not to have said that the flesh cannot be contrary to the spirit in any baptized person, as if I meant to imply that it is contrary in the unbaptized; but I ought to have made my statement general, to the effect that the flesh in no man's case is contrary. Now see into what a corner he drives himself. See what a man will say, who is unwilling to cry out with the apostle, "Who shall deliver me from the body of this death? The grace of God, through Jesus Christ our Lord." "But why," he asks, "should I so exclaim, who am already baptized in Christ? It is for them to cry out thus who have not yet received so great a benefit, whose words the apostle in a figure transferred to himself, —if indeed even they say so much." Well, this defense of nature does not permit even these to utter this exclamation! For in the baptized, there is no nature; and in the unbaptized, nature is not! Or if even in the one class it is allowed to be corrupted, so that it is not without reason that men exclaim, "O wretched man that I am! who shall deliver me from this body of death?" to the other, too, help is brought in what follows: "The grace of God, through Jesus Christ our Lord;" then let it at last be granted that human nature stands in need of Christ for its Physician.

Chapter 65 [LV.]— "This Body of Death," So Called from Its Defect, Not from Its Substance.

Now, I ask, when did our nature lose that liberty, which he craves to be given to him when he says: "Who shall liberate me?" For even he finds no fault with the substance of the flesh when he expresses his desire to be liberated from the body of this death, since the nature of the body, as well as of the soul, must be attributed to the good God as the author thereof. But what he speaks of undoubtedly concerns the offences of the body. Now from the body the death of the body separates us; whereas the offences contracted from the body remain, and their just punishment awaits them, as the rich man found in hell. From these it was that he was unable to liberate himself, who said: "Who shall liberate me from the body of this death?" But whensoever it was that he lost this liberty, at least there remains that "inseparable capacity" of nature, —he has the ability from natural resources, —he has the volition from free will. Why does he seek the sacrament of baptism? Is it because of past sins, in order that they may be forgiven, since they cannot be undone? Well, suppose you acquit and release a man on these terms, he must still utter the old cry; for he not only wants to be mercifully let off from punishment for past offences, but to be strengthened and fortified against sinning for the time to come. For he "delights in the law of God, after the inward man; but then he sees another law in his members, warring against the law of his mind." Observe, he sees that there is, not recollects that there was. It is a present pressure, not a past memory. And he sees the other law not only "warring," but even "bringing him into captivity to the law of sin, which is" (not which was) "in his members." Hence comes that cry of his: "O wretched man that I am! who shall liberate me from the body of this death?" Let him pray, let him entreat for the help of the mighty Physician. Why gainsay that prayer? Why cry down that entreaty? Why shall the unhappy suitor be hindered from begging for the mercy of Christ, —and that too by Christians? For, it was even they who were accompanying Christ that tried to prevent the blind man, by clamoring him down, from begging for light; but even amidst the din and throng of the gainsayers He hears the suppliant; whence the response: "The grace of God, through Jesus Christ out Lord."

Chapter 66. —The Works, Not the Substance, of the "Flesh" Opposed to the "Spirit."

Now if we secure even this concession from them, that unbaptized persons may implore the assistance of the Savior's grace, this is indeed no slight point against that fallacious assertion of the self-sufficiency of nature and of the power of free will. For he is not sufficient to himself who says, "O wretched man that I am! who shall liberate me?" Nor can he be said to have full liberty who still asks for liberation. [LVI.] But let us, moreover, see to this point also, whether they who are baptized do the good which they would, without any resistance from the lust of the flesh. That, however, which we must say on this subject, our author himself mentions, when concluding this topic he says: "As we remarked, the passage in which occur the words, 'The flesh lusted against the Spirit,' must needs have reference not to the substance, but to the works of the flesh." We too allege that this is spoken not of the substance of the flesh, but of its works, which proceed from carnal concupiscence, —in a word, from sin, concerning which we have this precept: "Not to let it reign in our mortal body, that we should obey it in the lusts thereof."

Chapter 67 [LVII.]—Who May Be Said to Be Under the Law.

But even our author should observe that it is to persons who have been already baptized that it was said: "The flesh lusted against the Spirit, and the Spirit against the flesh, so that ye cannot do the things that ye would." And lest he should make them slothful for the actual conflict, and should seem by this statement to have given them laxity in sinning, he goes on to tell them: "If ye be led of the Spirit, ye are no longer under the law." For that man is under the law, who, from fear of the punishment which the law threatens, and not from any love for righteousness, obliges himself to abstain from the work of sin, without being as yet free and removed from the desire of sinning. For it is in his very will that he is guilty, whereby he would prefer, if it were possible, that what he dreads should not exist, in order that he might freely do what he secretly desires. Therefore he says, "If ye be led of the Spirit, ye are not under the law,"—even the law which inspires fear, but gives not love. For this "love is shed abroad in our hearts," not by the letter of the law, but "by the Holy Ghost which is given unto us." This is the law of liberty, not of bondage; being the law of love, not of fear; and concerning it the Apostle James says: "Whoso looked into the perfect law of liberty." Whence he, too, no longer indeed felt terrified by God's law as a slave, but delighted in it in the inward man, although still seeing another law in his members warring against the law of his mind. Accordingly he here says: "If ye be led of the Spirit, ye are not under the law." So far, indeed, as any man is led by the Spirit, he is not under the law; because, so far as he rejoices in the law of God, he lives not in fear of the law, since "fear has torment," not joy and delight.

Chapter 68 [LVIII.]—Despite the Devil, Man May, by God's Help, Be Perfected.

If, therefore, we feel rightly on this matter, it is our duty at once to be thankful for what is already healed within us, and to pray for such further healing as shall enable us to enjoy full liberty, in that most absolute state of health which is incapable of addition, the perfect pleasure of God. For we do not deny that human nature can be without sin; nor ought we by any means to refuse to it the ability to become perfect, since we admit its capacity for progress, —by God's grace, however, through our Lord Jesus Christ. By His assistance we aver that it becomes holy and happy, by whom it was created in order to be so. There is accordingly an easy refutation of the objection which our author says is alleged by some against him: "The devil opposes us." This objection we also meet in entirely identical language with that which he uses in reply: "We must resist him, and he will flee. 'Resist the devil,' says the blessed apostle, 'and he will flee from you.' From which it may be observed, what his harming amounts to against those whom he flees; or what power he is to be understood as possessing, when he prevails only against those who do not resist him." Such language is my own also; for it is impossible to employ truer words. There is, however, this difference between us and them, that we, whenever the devil must be resisted, not only do not deny, but actually teach, that God's help must be sought; whereas they attribute so much power to will as to take away prayer from religious duty. Now it is certainly with a view to resisting the devil and his fleeing from us that we say when we pray, "Lead us not into temptation;" to the same end also are we warned by our Captain, exhorting us as soldiers in the words: "Watch ye and pray, lest ye enter into temptation."

Chapter 69 [LIX.]—Pelagius Puts Nature in the Place of Grace.

In opposition, however, to those who ask, "And who would be unwilling to be without sin, if it were put in the power of a man?" he rightly contends, saying "that by this very question they acknowledge that the thing is not impossible; because so much as this, many, if not all men, certainly desire." Well then, let him only confess how this is possible, and then our controversy is ended. Now the means is "the grace of God through our Lord Jesus Christ;" by which he nowhere has been willing to allow that we are assisted when we pray, for the avoidance of sin. If indeed he secretly allows this, he must forgive us if we suspect otherwise. For he himself works this result, who, though encountering so much obloquy on this subject, wishes to entertain the secret opinion, and yet is unwilling to confess or profess it. It would surely be no great matter were he to speak out, especially since he has undertaken to handle and open this point, as if it had been objected against him on the side of opponents. Why on such occasions did he choose only to defend nature, and assert that man was so created as to have it in his power not to sin if he wished not to sin; and, from the fact that he was so created, definitely say that the power was owing to God's grace which enabled him to avoid sin, if he was unwilling to commit it; and yet refuse to say anything concerning the fact that even nature itself is either, because disordered, healed by God's grace through our Lord Jesus Christ or else assisted by it, because in itself it is so insufficient?

Chapter 70 [LX.]—Whether Any Man is Without Sin in This Life.

Now, whether there ever has been, or is, or ever can be, a man living so righteous a life in this world as to have no sin at all, may be an open question among true and pious Christians; but whoever doubts the possibility of this sinless state after this present life; is foolish. For my own part, indeed, I am unwilling to dispute the point even as respects this life. For although that passage seems to me to be incapable of bearing any doubtful sense, wherein it is written, "In thy sight shall no man living be justified" (and so of similar passages), yet I could wish it were possible to show either that such quotations were capable of bearing a better signification, or that a perfect and plenary righteousness, to which it were impossible for any accession to be made, had been realized at some former time in someone whilst passing through this life in the flesh, or was now being realized, or would be hereafter. They, however, are in a great majority, who, while not doubting that to the last day of their life it will be needful to them to resort to the prayer which they can so truthfully utter, "Forgive us our trespasses, as we forgive those who trespass against us," still trust that in Christ and His promises they possess a true, certain, and unfailing hope. There is, however, no method whereby any persons arrive at absolute perfection, or whereby any man makes the slightest progress to true and godly righteousness, but the assisting grace of our crucified Savior Christ, and the gift of His Spirit; and whosoever shall deny this cannot rightly, I almost think, be reckoned in the number of any kind of Christians at all.

Chapter 71 [LXI.]—Augustin Replies Against the Quotations Which Pelagius Had Advanced Out of the Catholic Writers. Lactantius.

Accordingly, with respect also to the passages which he has adduced, —not indeed from the canonical Scriptures, but out of certain treatises of catholic writers, —I wish to meet the assertions of such as say that the said quotations make for him. The fact is, these passages are so entirely neutral, that they oppose neither our own opinion nor his. Amongst them he wanted to class something out of my own books, thus accounting me to be a person who seemed worthy of being ranked with them. For this I must not be ungrateful, and I should be sorry—so I say with unaffected friendliness—for him to be in error, since he has conferred this honor upon me. As for his first quotation, indeed, why need I examine it largely, since I do not see here the author's name, either because he has not given it, or because from some casual mistake the copy which you forwarded to me did not contain it? Especially as in writings of such authors I feel myself free to use my own judgment (owing unhesitating assent to nothing but the canonical Scriptures), whilst in fact there is not a passage which he has quoted from the works of this anonymous author that disturbs me. "It behooved," says he, "for the Master and Teacher of virtue to become most like to man, that by conquering sin He might show that man is able to conquer sin." Now, however this passage may be expressed, its author must see to it as to what explanation it is capable of bearing. We, indeed, on our part, could not possibly doubt that in Christ there was no sin to conquer, —born as He was in the likeness of sinful flesh, not in sinful flesh itself.

Another passage is adduced from the same author to this effect: "And again, that by subduing the desires of the flesh He might teach us that it is not of necessity that one sins, but of set purpose and will." For my own part, I understand these desires of the flesh (if it is not of its unlawful lusts that the writer here speaks) to be such as hunger, thirst, refreshment after fatigue, and the like. For it is through these, however faultless they be in themselves, that some men fall into sin, —a result which was far from our blessed Savior, even though, as we see from the evidence of the gospel, these affections were natural to Him owing to His likeness to sinful flesh.

Chapter 72 [LXI.]—Hilary. The Pure in Heart Blessed. The Doing and Perfecting of Righteousness.

He quotes the following words from the blessed Hilary: "It is only when we shall be perfect in spirit and changed in our immortal state, which blessedness has been appointed only for the pure in heart, that we shall see that which is immortal in God." Now I am really not aware what is here said contrary to our own statement, or in what respect this passage is of any use to our opponent, unless it be that it testifies to the possibility of a man's being "pure in heart." But who denies such possibility? Only it must be by the grace of God, through Jesus Christ our Lord, and not merely by our freedom of will. He goes on to quote also this passage: "This Job had so effectually read these Scriptures, that he kept himself from every wicked work, because he worshipped God purely with a mind unmixed with offences: now such worship of God is the proper work of righteousness." It is what Job had done which the writer here spoke of, not what he had brought to perfection in this world, —much less what he had done or perfected without the grace of that Savior whom he had actually foretold. For that man, indeed, abstains from every wicked work, who does not allow the sin which he has within him to have dominion over him; and who, whenever an unworthy thought stole over him, suffered it not to come to a head in actual deed. It is, however, one thing not to have sin, and another to refuse obedience to its desires. It is one thing to fulfil the command, "Thou shalt not covet;" and another thing, by an endeavor at any rate after abstinence, to do that which is also written, "Thou shalt not go after thy lusts." And yet one is quite aware that he can do nothing of all this without the Savior's grace. It is to work righteousness, therefore, to fight in an internal struggle with the internal evil of concupiscence in the true worship of God; whilst to perfect it means to have no adversary at all. Now he who must fight is still in danger, and is sometimes shaken, even if he is not overthrown; whereas he who has no enemy at all rejoices in perfect peace. He, moreover, is in the highest truth said to be without sin in whom no sin has an indwelling, —not he who, abstaining from evil deeds, uses such language as "Now it is no longer I that do it, but the sin that dwelleth in me."

Chapter 73. —He Meets Pelagius with Another Passage from Hilary.

Now even Job himself is not silent respecting his own sins; and your friend, of course, is justly of opinion that humility must not by any means "be put on the side of falsehood." Whatever confession, therefore, Job makes, inasmuch as he is a true worshipper of God, he undoubtedly makes it in truth. Hilary, likewise, while expounding that passage of the psalm in which it is written, "Thou hast despised all those who turn aside from Thy commandments," says: "If God were to despise sinners, He would despise indeed all men, because no man is without sin; but it is those who turn away from Him, whom they call apostates, that He despises." You observe his statement: it is not to the effect that no man was without sin, as if he spoke of the past; but no man is without sin; and on this point, as I have already remarked, I have no contention with him. But if one refuses to submit to the Apostle John, —who does not himself declare, "If we were to say we have had no sin," but "If we say we have no sin,"—how is he likely to show deference to Bishop Hilary? It is in defense of the grace of Christ that I lift up my voice, without which grace no man is justified, —just as if natural free will were sufficient. Nay, He Himself lifts up His own voice in defense of the same. Let us submit to Him when He says: "Without me ye can do nothing."

Chapter 74 [LXIII.]—Ambrose.

St. Ambrose, however, really opposes those who say that man cannot exist without sin in the present life. For, in order to support his statement, he avails himself of the instance of Zacharias and Elisabeth, because they are mentioned as "having walked in all the commandments and ordinances" of the law "blameless." Well, but does he for all that deny that it was by God's grace that they did this through our Lord Jesus Christ? It was undoubtedly by such faith in Him that holy men lived of old, even before His death. It is He who sends the Holy Ghost that is given to us, through whom that love is shed abroad in our hearts whereby alone whosoever are righteous are righteous. This same Holy Ghost the bishop expressly mentioned when he reminds us that He is to be obtained by prayer (so that the will is not sufficient unless it be aided by Him); thus in his hymn he says:

"Votisque præstat sedulis, Sanctum mereri Spiritum,"

— "To those who sedulously seek He gives to gain the Holy Spirit."

Chapter 75. —Augustin Adduces in Reply Some Other Passages of Ambrose.

I, too, will quote a passage out of this very work of St. Ambrose, from which our opponent has taken the statement which he deemed favorable for citation: "'It seemed good to me,'" he says; "but what he declares seemed good to him cannot have seemed good to him alone. For it is not simply to his human will that it seemed good, but also as it pleased Him, even Christ, who, says he, speaks in me, who it is that causes that which is good in itself to seem good to ourselves also. For him on whom He has mercy He also calls. He, therefore, who follows Christ, when asked why he wished to be a Christian, can answer: 'It seemed good to me.' In saying this he does not deny that it also pleased God; for from God proceeds the preparation of man's will inasmuch as it is by God's grace that God is honored by His saint." See now what your author must learn, if he takes pleasure in the words of Ambrose, how that man's will is prepared by God, and that it is of no importance, or, at any rate, does not much matter, by what means or at what time the preparation is accomplished, provided no doubt is raised as to whether the thing itself be capable of accomplishment without the grace of Christ. Then, again, how important it was that he should observe one line from the words of Ambrose which he quoted! For after that holy man had said, "Inasmuch as the Church has been gathered out of the world, that is, out of sinful men, how can it be unpolluted when composed of such polluted material, except that, in the first place, it be washed of sins by the grace of Christ, and then, in the next place, abstain from sins through its nature of avoiding sin?"—he added the following sentence, which your author has refused to quote for a self-evident reason; for [Ambrose] says: "It was not from the first unpolluted, for that was impossible for human nature: but it is through God's grace and nature that because it no longer sins, it comes to pass that it seems unpolluted." Now who does not understand the reason why your author declined adding these words? It is, of course, so contrived in the discipline of the present life, that the holy Church shall arrive at last at that condition of most immaculate purity which all holy men desire; and that it may in the world to come, and in a state unmixed with anything of evil men, and undisturbed by any law of sin resisting the law of the mind, lead the purest life in a divine eternity. Still he should well observe what Bishop Ambrose says, —and his statement exactly tallies with the Scriptures: "It was not from the first unpolluted, for that condition was impossible for human nature." By his phrase, "from the first," he means indeed from the time of our being born of Adam. Adam no doubt was himself created immaculate; in the case, however, of those who are by nature children of wrath, deriving from him what in him was corrupted, he distinctly averred that it was an impossibility in human nature that they should be immaculate from the first.

Chapter 76 [LXIV.]—John of Constantinople.

He quotes also John, bishop of Constantinople, as saying "that sin is not a substance, but a wicked act." Who denies this? "And because it is not natural, therefore the law was given against it, and because it proceeds from the liberty of our will." Who, too, denies this? However, the present question concerns our human nature in its corrupted state; it is a further question also concerning that grace of God whereby our nature is healed by the great Physician, Christ, whose remedy it would not need if it were only whole. And yet your author defends it as capable of not sinning, as if it were sound, or as if its freedom of will were self-sufficient.

Chapter 77. —Xystus.

What Christian, again, is unaware of what he quotes the most blessed Xystus, bishop of Rome and martyr of Christ, as having said, "God has conferred upon men liberty of their own will, in order that by purity and sinlessness of life they may become like unto God?" But the man who appeals to free will ought to listen and believe, and ask Him in whom he believes to give him His assistance not to sin. For when he speaks of "becoming like unto God," it is indeed through God's love that men are to be like unto God, —even the love which is "shed abroad in our hearts," not by any ability of nature or the free will within us, but "by the Holy Ghost which is given unto us." Then, in respect of what the same martyr further says, "A pure mind is a holy temple for God, and a heart clean and without sin is His best altar," who knows not that the clean heart must be brought to this perfection, whilst "the inward man is renewed day by day," but yet not without the grace of God through Jesus Christ our Lord? Again, when he says, "A man of chastity and without sin has received power from God to be a son of God," he of course meant it as an admonition that on a man's becoming so chaste and sinless (without raising any question as to where and when this perfection was to be obtained by him,—although in fact it is quite an interesting question among godly men, who are notwithstanding agreed as to the possibility of such perfection on the one hand, and on the other hand its impossibility except through "the one Mediator between God and men, the Man Christ Jesus");—nevertheless, as I began to say, Xystus designed his words to be an admonition that, on any man's attaining such a high character, and thereby being rightly reckoned to be among the sons of God, the attainment must not be thought to have been the work of his own power. This indeed he, through grace, received from God, since he did not have it in a nature which had become corrupted and depraved, — even as we read in the Gospel, "But as many as received Him, to them gave He power to become the sons of God;" which they were not by nature, nor could at all become, unless by receiving Him they also received power through His grace. This is the power which is claimed for itself by the fortitude of that love which is only communicated to us by the Holy Ghost bestowed upon us.

Chapter 78 [LXV.]—Jerome.

We have next a quotation of some words of the venerable presbyter Jerome, from his exposition of the passage where it is written: "'Blessed are the pure in heart; for they shall see God.' These are they whom no consciousness of sin reproves," he says, and adds: "The pure man is seen by his purity of heart; the temple of God cannot be defiled." This perfection is, to be sure, wrought in us by endeavor, by labor, by prayer, by effectual importunity therein that we may be brought to the perfection in which we may be able to look upon God with a pure heart, by His grace through our Lord Jesus Christ. As to his quotation, that the aforementioned presbyter said, "God created us with free will; we are drawn by necessity neither to virtue nor to vice; otherwise, where there is necessity there is no crown;" — who would not allow this? Who would not cordially accept it? Who would deny that human nature was so created? The reason, however, why in doing a right action there is no bondage of necessity, is that liberty comes of love.

Chapter 79 [LXVI.]—A Certain Necessity of Sinning.

But let us revert to the apostle's assertion: "The love of God is shed abroad in our hearts by the Holy Ghost which is given unto us." By whom given if not by Him who "ascended up on high, led captivity captive, and gave gifts unto men?" Forasmuch, however, as there is, owing to the defects that have entered our nature, not to the constitution of our nature, a certain necessary tendency to sin, a man should listen, and in order that the said necessity may cease to exist, learn to say to God, "Bring Thou me out of my necessities;" because in the very offering up of such a prayer there is a struggle against the tempter, who fights against us concerning this very necessity; and thus, by the assistance of grace through our Lord Jesus Christ, both the evil necessity will be removed and full liberty be bestowed.

Chapter 80 [LXVII.]—Augustin Himself. Two Methods Whereby Sins, Like Diseases, are Guarded Against.

Let us now turn to our own case. "Bishop Augustin also," says your author, "in his books on Free Will has these words: 'Whatever the cause itself of volition is, if it is impossible to resist it, submission to it is not sinful; if, however, it may be resisted, let it not be submitted to, and there will be no sin. Does it, perchance, deceive the unwary man? Let him then beware that he be not deceived. Is the deception, however, so potent that it is not possible to guard against it? If such is the case, then there are no sins. For who sins in a case where precaution is quite impossible? Sin, however, is committed; precaution therefore is possible.'" I acknowledge it, these are my words; but he, too, should condescend to acknowledge all that was said previously, seeing that the discussion is about the grace of God, which helps us as a medicine through the Mediator; not about the impossibility of righteousness. Whatever, then, may be the cause, it can be resisted. Most certainly it can. Now it is because of this that we pray for help, saying, "Lead us not into temptation," and we should not ask for help if we supposed that the resistance were quite impossible. It is possible to guard against sin, but by the help of Him who cannot be deceived. For this very circumstance has much to do with guarding against sin that we can unfeignedly say, "Forgive us our debt, as we forgive our debtors." Now there are two ways whereby, even in bodily maladies, the evil is guarded against, —to prevent its occurrence, and, if it happen, to secure a speedy cure. To prevent its occurrence, we may find precaution in the prayer, "Lead us not into temptation;" to secure the prompt remedy, we have the resource in the prayer, "Forgive us our debts." Whether then the danger only threatens or be inherent, it may be guarded against.

Chapter 81. —Augustin Quotes Himself on Free Will.

In order, however, that my meaning on this subject may be clear not merely to him, but also to such persons as have not read those treatises of mine on Free Will, which your author has read, and who have not only not read them, but perchance do read him; I must go on to quote out of my books what he has omitted, but which, if he had perceived and quoted in his book, no controversy would be left between us on this subject. For immediately after those words of mine which he has quoted, I expressly added, and (as fully as I could) worked out, the train of thought which might occur to any one's mind, to the following effect: "And yet some actions are disapproved of, even when they are done in ignorance, and are judged deserving of chastisement, as we read in the inspired authorities." After taking some examples out of these, I went on to speak also of infirmity as follows:

"Some actions also deserve disapprobation, that are done from necessity; as when a man wishes to act rightly and cannot. For whence arise those utterances: 'For the good that I would, I do not; but the evil which I would not, that I do'?" Then, after quoting some other passages of the Holy Scriptures to the same effect, I say: "But all these are the sayings of persons who are coming out of that condemnation of death; for if this is not man's punishment, but his nature, then those are no sins." Then, again, a little afterwards I add: "It remains, therefore, that this just punishment come of man's condemnation. Nor ought it to be wondered at, that either by ignorance man has not free determination of will to choose what he will rightly do, or that by the resistance of carnal habit (which by force of mortal transmission has, in a certain sense, become engrafted into his nature), though seeing what ought rightly to be done and wishing to do it, he yet is unable to accomplish it. For this is the most just penalty of sin, that a man should lose what he has been unwilling to make good use of, when he might with ease have done so if he would; which, however, amounts to this, that the man who knowingly does not do what is right loses the ability to do it when he wishes. For, in truth, to every soul that sins there accrue these two penal consequences— ignorance and difficulty. Out of the ignorance springs the error which disgraces; out of the difficulty arises the pain which afflicts. But to approve of falsehoods as if they were true, so as to err involuntarily, and to be unable, owing to the resistance and pain of carnal bondage, to refrain from deeds of lust, is not the nature of man as he was created, but the punishment of man as under condemnation. When, however, we speak of a free will to do what is right, we of course mean that liberty in which man was created." Some men at once deduce from this what seems to them a just objection from the transfer and transmission of sins of ignorance and difficulty from the first man to his posterity. My answer to such objectors is this: "I tell them, by way of a brief reply, to be silent and to cease from murmuring against God. Perhaps their complaint might have been a proper one, if no one from among men had stood forth a vanquisher of error and of lust; but when there is everywhere present One who calls off from himself, through the creature by so many means, the man who serves the Lord, teaches him when believing, consoles him when hoping, encourages him when loving, helps him when endeavoring, hears him when praying,—it is not reckoned to you as a fault that you are involuntarily ignorant, but that you neglect to search out what you are ignorant of; nor is it imputed to you in censure that you do not bind up the limbs that are wounded, but that you despise him who wishes to heal them." In such terms did I exhort them, as well as I could, to live righteously; nor did I make the grace of God of none effect, without which the now obscured and tarnished nature of man can neither be enlightened nor purified. Our whole discussion with them on this subject turns upon this, that we frustrate not the grace of God which is in Jesus Christ our Lord by a perverted assertion of nature. In a passage occurring shortly after the last quoted one, I said in reference to nature: "Of nature itself we speak in one sense, when we properly describe it as that human nature in which man was created faultless after his kind; and in another sense as that nature in which we are born ignorant and carnally minded, owing to the penalty of condemnation, after the manner of the apostle, 'We ourselves likewise were by nature children of wrath, even as others.'"

Chapter 82 [LXVIII.]—How to Exhort Men to Faith, Repentance, and Advancement.

If, therefore, we wish "to rouse and kindle cold and sluggish souls by Christian exhortations to lead righteous lives," we must first of all exhort them to that faith whereby they may become Christians, and be subjects of His name and authority, without whom they cannot be saved. If, however, they are already Christians but neglect to lead holy lives, they must be chastised with alarms and be aroused by the praises of reward,—in such a manner, indeed, that we must not forget to urge them to godly prayers as well as to virtuous actions, and furthermore to instruct them in such wholesome doctrine that they be induced thereby to return thanks for being able to accomplish any step in that holy life which they have entered upon, without difficulty, and whenever they do experience such "difficulty," that they then wrestle with God in most faithful and persistent prayer and ready works of mercy to obtain from Him facility. But provided they thus progress, I am not over-anxious as to the where and the when of their perfection in fulness of righteousness; only I solemnly assert, that wheresoever and whensoever they become perfect, it cannot be but by the grace of God through our Lord Jesus Christ. When, indeed, they have attained to the clear knowledge that they have no sin, let them not say they have sin, lest the truth be not in them; even as the truth is not in those persons who, though they have sin, yet say that they have it not.

Chapter 83 [LXIX.]—God Enjoins No Impossibility, Because All Things are Possible and Easy to Love.

But "the precepts of the law are very good," if we use them lawfully. Indeed, by the very fact (of which we have the firmest conviction) "that the just and good God could not possibly have enjoined impossibilities," we are admonished both what to do in easy paths and what to ask for when they are difficult. Now all things are easy for love to effect, to which (and which alone) "Christ's burden is light,"—or rather, it is itself alone the burden which is light. Accordingly it is said, "And His commandments are not grievous;" so that whoever finds them grievous must regard the inspired statement about their "not being grievous" as having been capable of only this meaning, that there may be a state of heart to which they are not burdensome, and he must pray for that disposition which he at present wants, so as to be able to fulfil all that is commanded him. And this is the purport of what is said to Israel in Deuteronomy, if understood in a godly, sacred, and spiritual sense, since the apostle, after quoting the passage, "The word is nigh thee, even in thy mouth and in thy heart" (and, as the verse also has it, in thine hands, for in man's heart are his spiritual hands), adds in explanation, "This is the word of faith which we preach." No man, therefore, who "returns to the Lord his God," as he is there commanded, "with all his heart and with all his soul," will find God's commandment "grievous." How, indeed, can it be grievous, when it is the precept of love? Either, therefore, a man has not love, and then it is grievous; or he has love, and then it is not grievous. But he possesses love if he does what is there enjoined on Israel, by returning to the Lord his God with all his heart and with all his soul. "A new commandment," says He, "do I give unto you, that ye love one another;" and "He that loveth his neighbor hath fulfilled the law;" and again, "Love is the fulfilling of the law." In accordance with these sayings is that passage, "Had they trodden good paths, they would have found, indeed, the ways of righteousness easy." How then is it written, "Because of the words of Thy lips, I have kept the paths of difficulty," except it be that both statements are true: These paths are paths of difficulty to fear; but to love they are easy?

Chapter 84 [LXX.]—The Degrees of Love are Also Degrees of Holiness.

Inchoate love, therefore, is inchoate holiness; advanced love is advanced holiness; great love is great holiness; "perfect love is perfect holiness,"—but this "love is out of a pure heart, and of a good conscience, and of faith unfeigned," "which in this life is then the greatest, when life itself is contemned in comparison with it." I wonder, however, whether it has not a soil in which to grow after it has quitted this mortal life! But in what place and at what time soever it shall reach that state of absolute perfection, which shall admit of no increase, it is certainly not "shed abroad in our hearts" by any energies either of the nature or the volition that are within us, but "by the Holy Ghost which is given unto us," "and which both helps our infirmity and co-operates with our strength. For it is itself indeed the grace of God, through our Lord Jesus Christ, to whom, with the Father and the Holy Spirit, appertained eternity, and all goodness, for ever and ever.

Amen.

www.ingramcontent.com/pod-product-compliance
Lightning Source LLC
Chambersburg PA
CBHW052106070526
44584CB00017B/2359